Wives of

the Warriors

Wives of the Warriors

Living Confidently in Christ

Ronda Sturgill

Pleasant Word
A Division of WINEPRESS PUBLISHING

Printed in the United States of America

Packaged by Pleasant Word, a Division of WinePress Publishing, PO Box 428, Enumclaw, WA 98022. The views expressed or implied in this work do not necessarily reflect those of WinePress Publishing. The author(s) is ultimately responsible for the design, content, and editorial accuracy of this work.

Unless otherwise noted, Scripture quotations in this book are taken from the Holy Bible, New International Version, Copyright © 1973, 1978, 1984 by the International Bible Society. Used by permission of Zondervan Publishing House. The "NIV" and "New International Version" trademarks are registered in the United States Patent and Trademark Office by International Bible Society.

ISBN 1-57921-532-7
Library of Congress Catalog Card Number: 2002115812

Acknowledgements

There are several people I must thank by name for the assistance they gave me in completing this Bible Study. One person alone rarely accomplishes a project such as this.

At the time of this writing God surrounded me with a group of women who not only continuously encouraged me in this work, but actually helped me in the different areas involved with its completion. I want to extend my deepest and sincere thanks to the following people:

Joy Dunlap, a fellow Christian author and speaker, who wisely directed me to write this study in the first place. Her background in publicity and marketing enabled her to give me more ideas and suggestions for printing and publication than I could possibly carry out.

Lynn Torrenti, RE coordinator at Langley AFB. Her continual encouragement and willingness to design and print promotional materials was always appreciated.

Pam Dannon, a fellow PWOC Board Member, who kindly offered to edit this work. Her editorial skills match those of any publisher.

Donna Anderson and Clara Rigleman for reviewing this manuscript and making great suggestions for its improvement.

My prayer team: Charlie Sparkman, Richard Roberts and Dave Wininger, all strong, Godly men who have a heart for un-reached and unsaved airmen at Langley AFB. This project would have not been completed without the support of their faithful prayers.

Judy Pfender, a fellow Christian speaker whose light truly shines for the glory of God, for her continual prayers for my writing and speaking ministry.

My son Toby, for his "Way to go, Mom!" style of encouragement. His level of maturity and love for God reaches far beyond his young age of twenty years.

Finally, I must thank my own 'warrior'—my husband, Tim, whose Godly wisdom is woven throughout this entire study. His constant support of my writing and speaking ministry keeps me falling more and more in love with him each and every day!

To all of you, THANK YOU VERY MUCH!

Table of Contents

Introduction

*A*s the wife of a United States Air Force chaplain, I thoroughly enjoy the wonderful privilege I have to serve both God and my country. Coming from a small church nestled deep in the foothills of the Appalachian mountains of Southwest VA, I was totally unaware of the scope and significance my husband's ministry would play in support of our armed forces as they protect the freedoms we so much enjoy today.

Along with this freedom however, comes a price; a price that is paid for by everyone whose loved ones serve in the United States Armed Forces. Although military life consists of many blessings, its hardships are unique to none other, both during times of war and peace.

During peacetime we face moving every few years, extended separations from spouses, parents and siblings, loss of jobs, loss of friends, loss of everything familiar to us. Starting over again and again becomes a commonplace event for the military family.

During times of war we face the constant uncertainty of the safety of our loved one. More often than not, the exact location of our warrior is withheld from us and we are never told when they will be home. No one is more affected by these situations than the wives of the warriors.

I quickly learned if I am going to survive a lifetime of rapidly changing, uncertain circumstances I must have one constant in my life. The Lord Jesus Christ is that constant! Our needs for security, belonging, faith, fun and pleasure, self-worth, health and knowledge are periodically challenged as boxes and belongings get packed up and shipped off to parts unknown to us. If there is anything good to say about the externals in our life always changing, it makes us cling to what we know will remain internally steadfast.

God's word tells us we have been given fullness in Christ; in Him we are complete. As we move around from place to place, as my husband is called upon to serve out of country during wartime, I can think of no greater security than to know God is all I need; anywhere, anytime. I'm reminded of the Psalmist who once wrote, "In Him our souls will be satisfied as with the richest of foods." (Psalm 63:5) Once we find wholeness, completeness and satisfaction in Christ, we can confidently face our constantly changing environment.

Our completeness in Christ enables us to accept the purpose for which our spouses serve in the United States Armed Forces: to defend our country and our freedoms. Unfortunately, this involves warfare. In the times when my warrior has gone off to war, although lonely for conversation and a hug, I am complete in Christ. My completeness in Christ allows me to give my husband my total support and unconditional love, freeing him to concentrate on his ministry and to accomplish the tasks God sent him to accomplish.

In the first chapter of the book of Joshua we read about wives and children staying safely behind, while the 'fighting men, fully armed' go off to conquer the land God had given the Israelites. Not much has changed in the past thousands of years for those who are involved in warfare! The Lord's words to Joshua, "Be strong and courageous" are just as relevant to us today as they were back then.

Wives and children are still left behind, while our 'fighting men, fully armed' go off to conquer foreign lands. It's during these times when our lives are most affected by our husband's vocation. The long and sometimes dangerous duty assignments are extremely stressful for everyone.

Wives are suddenly put in the position of being a single parent, a difficult position to be in when we are happily married. The running of the household is left completely up to us. This is especially challenging for those who are extremely dependent upon their husbands. Work schedules, along with kid's schedules can be somewhat overwhelming when we are used to sharing those responsibilities. It's very tempting to transfer our frustrations directly onto our husbands.

We have to constantly remember our warriors feel helpless enough just being on the other side of the world! The more we can take responsibility to 'keeping the home fires burning,' the more we are doing our part to support our husband's military mission.

I will never become a military member, engaging in dangerous duty activities to defend our freedoms. So I view taking on more responsibility at home as a service to both my husband and my country, thankful I live in the United States of America.

The wives of our warriors have a very special need for belonging and becoming part of a body of believers. Meeting this need is critical to our growth and development as Christians. I find tremendous security in knowing at every military base there is a Chapel in which to worship. The women's Bible studies offered at military bases around the world are excellent tools God uses to give us a sense of belonging and companionship, while teaching us more about Him.

I'm convinced as we spend time with other believers, God weaves our lives together in such a fashion that those to whom we need to minister will be placed directly in front of us, along with those from whom we need to receive counsel. As our warriors are often deployed and wives are left alone to care for children, the friendships we share with our sisters in Christ are extremely important.

The cackling and laughter that often erupts has raised many a rooftop as we delight in each other's sense of humor. "Our mouths were filled with laughter, our tongues with songs of joy." (Psalm 126:2) There is definitely joy in knowing God, even when our husbands are far, far away.

As Christians we realize our significance lies in who we are in Christ and not who we are in the eyes of the world. Moving frequently causes us to refrain from looking to other people to determine our self-worth. New places where I don't know anyone is one of the hardest things I have to get used to. God uses this every time to teach me my significance lies in Christ, not in the eyes of other people.

Our knowledge of God and faith in Him continually increases as we see God meet these various needs in different ways at each location. Every assignment is another opportunity for Him to be faithful. We only experience His faithfulness to the degree we need Him to be faithful. Because I have needed Him to be faithful during the past sixteen years, I see Him more clearly as He constantly and graciously provides.

Lastly, being the wife of a warrior keeps me in a state of prayer. Paul tells us to pray at all times, to be in constant prayer, and to pray without ceasing. Without prayer, it is impossible to live victorious, powerful lives. I find tremendous peace in that Jesus is 'the Lord of Peace himself' and gives us peace at all times. This peace comes only through time spent in prayer.

When we began our journey as members of the United States Air Force sixteen years ago, I had no idea we were about to embark on a ministry that would be global. God has been more than faithful, causing our ministry to be fruitful, more than trustworthy, causing our ministry to be a testimony, and above all, more than gracious, causing our ministry to bring Him glory.

About This Study

$\mathcal{W}$*ives of the Warriors: Living Confidently in Christ* is a ten week Bible Study specifically designed for but not limited to the very unique needs of the wives of warriors on a spiritual level. The Biblical principles in this study can be applied to anyone's life in general, however the illustrations are written with specific applicability to the wives or spouses of our active duty military personnel.

Interaction with Scripture is a predominant theme throughout this study. We learn how to apply Biblical principles to our lives on a daily basis, making Scripture very real and practical. The principles we will study, when applied to our lives, enable us not to just survive some of the hardships we face as being wives of warriors, but to actually thrive in them. We can face our challenges living confidently in Christ.

The core of this study revolves around the principle, '*We are complete in Christ.*' Building upon that principle, I will introduce a new principle each week as we discover the true meaning of being '*full in Christ*' and how that relates to our lives as wives of warriors.

The following topics are addressed:

- God's grace and how it works in our lives
- God's plan for moving His people from place to place

- How God works through our weakness
- Forgiving by faith and not by feelings
- Running our race with perseverance
- The Biblical perspective of suffering
- The protection of the believer in Spiritual warfare
- Unity in diversity
- Experiencing God's power

The five-day format for this study is as follows:

DAY ONE: **PRAISE**

> o   We will spend the first day of each week interacting with Scriptures that will lead us into praise and worship.

DAY TWO: **THE PRINCIPLE**

> o   We will be presented with the Biblical principle along with its Scriptural background, based on one principle Bible verse.

DAY THREE AND FOUR: **PROOF OF THE PRINCIPLE**

> o   We will study Scripture that illustrates the principle along with how God used it in the lives of His people to accomplish His purposes.

DAY FIVE: **PRAISE AND PRACTICUM**

> o   We will end our week interacting with Scripture that will lead us into praise and worship as we contemplate how to apply the principle we have just studied to our own lives.

Ladies, thank you for joining me in this study. It is my deepest prayer that God will reveal Himself to you in a new and exciting way, making your life as a wife of a warrior a fruitful one as you serve God, as you serve your family and as you serve your country. Be thankful for the freedom we have to worship God anywhere at anytime and know you play a very important part in protecting that freedom.

May God continue to bless you, wives of the warriors, as you continue to live confidently in Christ.

Week One

Complete In Christ

"For in Christ all the fullness of the Diety lives in bodily form, and you have been given fullness in Christ."

COLOSSIANS 2:9,10

For the first week of our study we are going to start with the Biblical Principle upon which the rest of this study is written: *'We are complete in Christ.'* There is nothing more critical in the Christian life than to have a clear understanding of our completeness in Christ. If we are going to live as wives of the warriors, grasping this truth and applying it to our lives is essential. It will make the difference between living a life of desperate frustration and experiencing the abundant life Christ came to give to us.

In my seminars, I always use this simple chart to help people understand our actions are directly related to our knowledge and understanding. This principle can be applied to any area of our lives.

Knowledge and Understanding

↓

Beliefs Attitudes Actions

What this chart says is that our knowledge and understanding will determine our beliefs, which will determine our attitudes, which will in turn determine our actions. Simply put, our knowledge and understanding determines how we are going to act.

For instance, my knowledge and understanding of most sports is fairly minimal. My husband would probably say it is non-existent! It is this lack of understanding that affects my actions and causes me to spend as little time as possible watching sports on TV. Give me something I know and understand, and my actions will be completely different.

Knowing and understanding who we are 'in Christ' determines our beliefs which determine our attitudes which determine our actions. When we come to know we are complete in Christ, our souls flourish and our actions show it.

I pray God will reveal to you your completeness in Him through the Scriptures this week, and as He does, show you how to apply this truth to your everyday lives. As wives of warriors, once we find wholeness, completeness and satisfaction in Him, we can face our constantly changing environment; we can deal with the hardships that come as the price for our precious freedom; and we can support our husbands as they continue to serve in the United States Armed Forces.

Let's begin our study!

DAY ONE: PRAISE

For our praise and worship time throughout the course of this study, we will read Scripture *interactively*. What I mean *by interactively* is that we verbally respond very specifically to each verse. For example, Psalm

Sept. 6-7 '09

146:2 reads, 'I will praise the Lord all my life; I will sing praise to my God as long as I live.' (NIV)

You might respond to this verse by saying, "Yes Lord, I will praise you for as long as I live. I praise you for what you have done in the past (perhaps you could mention something specific) and I praise you for what you are doing in my life today." (Again, mention something specific.)

Interacting with Scripture in this manner teaches us to apply Scripture to our daily lives and helps us grasp the truth that God is interested in every detail. At various intervals, stop and remain silent while meditating on God's word. Just as we interact with Him, He also interacts with us in our moments of quiet.

Continue to read Psalm 146 and Psalms 19:7–11 interactively and then answer the following questions.

1. Read Psalm 146

    - What does the psalmist say about putting our trust in men?
    - From this psalm, how does our completeness in Christ meet the practical needs of people?
    - From what does He set the prisoner free?
    - What does God do for the depressed and downhearted?
    - How does it make you feel to know the Maker of Heaven and Earth also makes you complete?

2. Read Psalm 19:7–11

    - What is it that the Psalmist finds so fulfilling?
    - Describe how this fulfills him.
    - What are the Psalmist's final conclusions of the ways of the Lord?
    - Has God stirred your heart to be just as excited about Him as this psalmist?

I pray you have spent the past 20–30 minutes interacting with God, meditating on His word and simply basking in His love and presence. The more time we spend interacting with Scripture that leads us into praise and worship, the more He fills us and makes us complete. We discover that His Word really is more precious than gold, than much pure gold, and much, much sweeter than honey from the comb! (NIV Psalm 19:10)

DAY TWO: THE PRINCIPLE

The Biblical principle we will study this week is: *'We are complete in Christ.'*

1. Read Colossians 2:6–15.

    *   Note how many times this passage of Scripture mentions either 'in Him' or 'in Christ.'

Whenever we tell our children something very important we don't want them to forget, we usually tell them over and over again. Paul uses the same technique in these verses. He repeats the phrase 'in Him' or 'in Christ' over and over again in order to make a very important point. Paul wanted the people of Colosse to know exactly who they were and what they had been given in Christ.

The Greek translation for this phrase is, *'a primary preposition denoting a fixed position.'* (Strong) In other words, we are situated in Christ. Christians have a new permanent and fixed position. We would be wise to take a closer look at what Paul is saying to the people of Colosse by telling them they are already complete by being permanently situated in Christ.

To begin to understand what it means to have been given fullness in Christ, we must first do a word study on the word *'fullness.'* I know word studies can become tedious, however, they are critical to our understanding exactly what the author means by using a particular word.

And remember, the more we increase our understanding, the more our attitudes and actions will be affected.

The Greek word used for *fullness* in the New Testament is *'Pleroo'* and is derived from *'Pletho.' 'Pletho'* means *"to be fulfilled, lacking nothing, perfect, to fill to the top so that nothing shall be wanting."* (Strong) Paul was telling the people of Colosse they were complete, full, filled to the top with Christ. They lacked nothing. Christ was all they needed. The word picture painted here is so abundantly clear.

Pretend that you have a full cup of flour in your hands. Is there any room for anything else? The same concept is applied to the meaning of 'fullness in Christ.' When our lives are full with Christ, there is no room for anything else. Christ is all we need.

In order to put this principle of fullness in Christ in its proper context, we must look at previous verses to determine why Paul told this principle of fullness in Christ over and over again to this group of believers. Perhaps it was because they had such a difficult time grasping this truth.

2. <u>Read verse 8 closely</u>.

- List the things on which the people of Colosse were focused, rather than on Christ.

Clearly, this group needed to hear this message! The people of Colosse were focused on many other things, rather than on Christ. They were being drawn into believing hollow and deceptive philosophies of that time. They initially came to Christ in faith, but now they believed they needed to comply with human regulations such as circumcision, eating and drinking, and observing religious festivals.

They began to blend the Gospel of Christ with pagan religions. These religions were steeped in human traditions. They were also full of false teachings that led Christians away from Christ; there was a 'secret knowledge' that was to be sought after in places other than in Christ.

They began to depend on the basic principles of the world. They kept trying to make their lives complete by adding to it. The Ch of Colosse were seeking to find value and significance in such ceremonies, strict regulations, and celestial creations. The cult time told them they needed more than Christ. They neede gions, more religious ceremonies, more 'externals.' They v their freedom in Christ only to live in bondage according to the principles of the world.

This type of thinking is not much different from today's Western culture. The basic principles of the world we live in tell us everyday we need more than Christ to make us complete. We need more than Christ to give us value and significance. We need 'externals' to fulfill us.

In addition to Christ, we need designer clothes; we need the latest electronic gizmos and gadgets; we need to drive fancy cars and live in big, fancy houses. We need important, powerful jobs; we need physical health; we need spouses; we need children.

Picture again the full cup of flour you are holding in your hand. If you are going to put something else in the cup, what must you do with the existing flour? You must take some flour out in order to make room to put something else in it.

The same principle applies to our lives. Our lives are already full with Christ. If we feel as though we need something more to make us complete; i.e. 'externals,' the first thing we must do is to make room for them. We must take Christ out. We must reduce Christ in us. When our lives are not full with Christ, we have some empty spaces we desperately try to fill up with something else.

Sometimes this includes our marriages. When most of us get married, we have empty spaces or needs that our spouse unknowingly is expected to fulfill. We fall in love, not because we love our spouses unconditionally, but because they meet our needs.

As the years go by, a healthy marital relationship will enter into the stage of differentiation. This is where true marital growth takes place. We learn to love and accept each other for who they are and not for who we want them to be. We begin to find our security and significance in Christ, rather than in each other.

Our completeness in Christ is what enables us to love our husbands freely and unconditionally. We will never receive from our spouse that which we can only receive from Jesus. When we come to this realization, we no longer put unrealistic demands on our husbands. We are free to love them as God made them.

At times we, like the Colossians, depend upon the basic principles of this world rather than on Christ to make us complete. Any time we look to something else to bring value to our lives instead of Christ, we enter into a form of idol worship.

(An idol is anything that draws people away from God. An inadequate substitute for the love and presence of God, we often turn to our idols to find comfort and compassion.)

(The worldly things we seem to think we need to add to our lives in order to make us complete become our idols. Our positions in life, our material possessions, our pastime pleasures, can all become far too important to us. They can become our idols if we are not careful. Just as the people of Colosse put too much value on more religion, we can put too much value on more things.)

3.   Read Habakkuk 2:18–20; Jeremiah 2:1–5

- Describe an idol as pictured here.
- Are they of any value to us?
- Are there any idols we worship today that fall into these categories?

Notice Habakkuk calls idols, 'images that teach lies.' I can't help but think of the images we see everyday on television, in the movies, on magazine covers. In Jeremiah, we can hear the pain in God's voice as He asks the Israelites, "Did I not love you enough? What fault did you find in me that made you turn away?"

How can we avoid the temptation to look elsewhere other than to Christ for our completeness, for our security and significance?

4.   Read Colossians 2:6,7

- What does it mean to be rooted in something?
- What does it mean to be built up and strengthened in the faith?
- Notice this verse reads, 'as you were taught.'
- What does this mean to you?
- With what are we to overflow?

We can avoid the temptations of looking elsewhere for our completeness by being rooted and grounded in the Word. We cannot know God and His truth apart from spending time with Him. The more time we spend with Him being strengthened in the faith, the more we will be able to resist the hollow and deceptive philosophies that lead us away from Christ.

It is very important here that you do not misunderstand me. The externals I mentioned previously are not bad things in themselves to have. They are all wonderful blessings, blessings God wants to give to believers.

Our spouses, our families, our friends, our jobs, our activities, our material possessions, are all given to us by God out of His love, compassion and grace. When we seek Him first and find our satisfaction in Him and in Him alone, all these things will be added unto us. (Matthew 6:33)

It is when we seek completion from these externals instead of from being in Christ that we tend to lose our balance. Our priorities are backwards. Any satisfaction these externals bring will be temporary at best.

Praise God He makes us complete! We have been given everything we need to live a purposeful, satisfying and fulfilled life. In Him, we lack nothing! As the Psalmist rejoices in Psalm 23, let's join him in proclaiming our cup overflows with God's goodness and love.

Today, we've looked at the meaning of fullness in Christ. We've seen how being complete in Christ affects our relationship with our husbands by freeing us to love them unconditionally. We've looked at the trappings and fallibility of idol worship and the consequences we face when we fill our lives with things other than Christ. And we've looked at the importance of being rooted and grounded in our faith. Tomorrow, we will look at the blessings we are given by our fullness in Christ; blessings that enable us to live each day joyfully, no matter what our circumstances.

DAY THREE AND FOUR: PROOF OF THE PRINCIPLE

Before we begin to take a close look at the proof of this week's principle, *'We are complete in Christ,'* we must first make the choice to believe God's word. When it tells us something is ours, we must believe it. We have a tendency to think if our blessings are not tangible and if the circumstances of our lives seem to contradict God's promises to us, then God's word must not be true.

Please do not allow yourself to be drawn into this type of thinking! Our completeness in Christ is a spiritual blessing rather than a physical or material blessing. Therefore, we must think of our fullness in Christ in spiritual terms.

When we think of our fullness in Christ in spiritual terms, we must realize much of the work of God is invisible; we are knit together and by the grace of his covenant are one with Christ. We become one 'in Christ' and Christ becomes one 'in us.' Our old self is dead and our new life is now hidden with Christ, invisibly enmeshed by the working of the Holy Spirit. We will study this union in greater detail in Chapter Ten.

As we claim our fullness in Christ, the mark that is left on us is internal, not external. Our circumstances may not change, but the attitude of our hearts will. We will desire to know Him more and to live our lives in a manner worthy of our calling.

Let's take a look at the blessings that are ours because we are complete in Christ.

1. <u>Read again Colossians 2:11–15</u>

   - List the spiritual blessings that you find in these verses using the following verses as a cross reference: Romans 6:6, 18; Romans 8:9; 2 Corinthians 3:17; Ephesians 2:13; 1 Peter 2:24; 1 John 1:9; Ephesians 1:19–22.

In these verses that follow our principle verse, Colossians 2:10, I find four very specific blessings that are ours as a result of us being complete in Christ.

   1. *Our sinful nature has been broken off!*

      The word 'circumcise' means, '*to cut around*'. Spiritually, our sinful nature has been cut off of us by Christ! Although once controlled by our sinful nature, we now are free to be controlled by the Holy Spirit. Where the Spirit of the Lord is, there is true freedom. This does not mean that we will never sin again, but it does mean that we are no longer slaves to sin. Sin no longer rules our lives. As wives of warriors, we no longer have to live with fear, worry and anxiety, but rather we have the freedom to choose hope and peace by trusting in a loving God.

2. *We are brought into an intimate relationship with Christ!*

    Spiritually, we have been buried with Christ and raised with Him. Once separated and far from God, we are now made alive with Christ. Through Christ's death and resurrection, we can enjoy an intimate relationship with our Heavenly Father. Ephesians 3:17 tells us that Christ dwells in our hearts by faith.

3. *We are forgiven of all our sins!*

    Jesus became our sin for us and so therefore, our sin was nailed to the cross! We no longer have to pay the penalty of not being able to keep the law, but rather we now live by grace! Through Christ, God canceled the written code. There are no longer laws that bind us. Instead, we can stand before God, righteous and holy, free from sin and without accusation! Because of this forgiveness, we can live our lives in freedom, according to God's will.

4. *God has disarmed Satan and deprived his cohorts of power!*

    We are victorious over our Spiritual enemy simply by who we are in Christ. God has taken away any power that he once had. The King James translation uses the word *'spoiled,'* meaning, *'denoting separation from what is put off.'* (Strong) Satan has been put off and separated from us. God stands in that gap, making a spectacle of him while triumphing over him. All things have been placed under God's feet. This includes our adversary.

Let's see what other blessings are ours because we are complete in Christ.

2. <u>Read the following verses and list the blessings of being complete in Christ</u>.

- John 14:27; Psalms 29:11
- Romans 8:28; Psalm 18:30–32
- Romans 8:15,16; Galatians 3:26
- Romans 8:29; 2 Corinthians 3:18
- Romans 8:26; John 14:16,17
- Romans 8:35–39; Ephesians 3:17–19

One of the blessings of our completeness in Christ is a life of peace. When we are in Christ, we experience an inner rest. The peace Jesus gives us is very real and personal. Ephesians 2:14 says, "For he himself is our peace." Particularly in our times of difficulty, it's often this peace that sustains us.

We have been given the blessing of peace in our fullness in Christ, but nothing will take away that blessing faster than trying to control our own lives for our own purposes and benefits. When we try to de-throne God as the ruler of our lives, we will forfeit our blessing of peace.

Our mind is the battleground where the struggle between our flesh and spirit is played out. When our minds are set on the temporal things of the earth, we bring unrest into our lives. We always feel like we have come up short. However, when we walk according to the fullness He has given us, we experience a peace that passes all understanding.

Our fullness in Christ means we become children of God. Christians become adopted Sons of God by grace, and are promised to share in the spiritual inheritances along with Christ. The concept of adoption in this Scripture is no different than that which we know it to be true in the world today. Adopted children become part of the family and enjoy parent/child relationships with their adopted parents, equally privy to all of the blessings of their natural born children. In Christ, we too, live as a child of God and can enjoy an intimate relationship with our Heavenly Father.

In Christ we have been given a prayer helper. When we don't know how to pray or have just become too weary to pray, the Spirit takes over for us. Sometimes we have prayed so hard and so long for something we have not yet received or seen evidence of, we no longer know how to ask. The Holy Spirit guides us in our prayer life and intercedes on our behalf and the others for whom we are praying. Since the Spirit is all knowing, he guides our hearts to ask for that which is God's will.

When we are complete in Christ we take on a new perspective of our lives. Where once we may have been thrown into the depths of despair over some circumstances in our lives, we now know there is a purpose for all things. This does not mean we will not experience some distressing of the soul as we encounter hardships or that we will understand everything that happens to us.

Christians will always face the similar hardships of unbelievers: illnesses and what seems to be 'untimely deaths' of loved ones, financial difficulties, losses of one kind or another. The difference between the believer and the non-believer is the believer's reaction to them and God's use of them. I address this issue in greater detail in Chapter Seven—Suffering: Hurting and Healing.

Fullness in Christ gives us a new goal: to become more like Jesus. Think about it . . . "conformed to the likeness of His son." We are supposed to become just like Jesus! That's a pretty tall order for most of us!

We are to take on the mind and attitude of Jesus by clothing ourselves with compassion, kindness, humility, gentleness and patience. Everybody has heard of the phrase, "What Would Jesus Do?" I prefer to ask the question, "What did Jesus do?" Since Jesus was fully human, he has set the standard of Godly behavior.

Our participation in this process is vital. We must cooperate with God. Becoming like Christ doesn't just happen automatically; it's something that takes time. Although we will never reach the level of sinless perfection of Jesus, we are being transformed and renewed each and every moment we spend in His Word and with Him in prayer.

The most important blessing of being complete in Christ is the security of God's love. When we know nothing will separate us from the love of God, we are free to live our lives without fear. No matter what our circumstances, whether they are terrific or tragic, we know we will never be separated from God.

He has given us peace. He has given us a Helper. He calls us His children. He has given us a new goal. He has assured us His love. Yes, in Him, we are complete. We need nothing more than what we have already been given.

3. Read Ephesians 1: 3–8

    • How many blessings has He blessed us with?

- Are these blessings physical or spiritual?
- What is God's purpose for us as believers?
- In addition to the blessings we've already studied, what blessings are mentioned here?
- According to what are these blessings given?
- Is God stingy or generous in the outpouring of His grace?

We have spent the past two days studying the blessings we have received as the result of us being complete in Christ. These blessings are internal, rather than external; spiritual, rather than physical. However, as our knowledge and understanding of these blessings increase, it will be reflected externally in our attitudes and actions.

The once unthinkable, long separations from our husbands; the frequent moves; the kids changing schools; leaving behind jobs and friends, all become 'do-able' situations as we grasp the truth that we are complete in Christ. Our completeness in Christ includes a promise from Him to meet each and every one of our needs.

In his letter to the Colossians, Paul pleads with them to accept their completeness and to look only to God; to put away all other forms of worship. In Him they are complete, nothing is lacking. In Him there is sufficiency for all things. They need not look any farther and neither must we. When we are able to grasp the truth that in Him our lives are complete, we can indeed live more confidently as wives of warriors!

DAY FIVE: PRAISE AND PRACTICUM

Let's finish up the week with another time of reading Scripture interactively. Thank God for how He revealed himself to you this week through His Word and ask Him to show you how you can apply it to your life.

1. <u>Read Psalm 115</u>

- To whom are we to give glory and why?
- What do these verses say about idols and those who find completeness in them?
- What does God promise for those who trust in Him?
- What does God promise you as you trust Him?

Our next assignment for today is to apply the Biblical principle we have studied this week to our own life.

2. Spend a few reflective moments with the Savior and ask Him, "In what areas do I need to believe that I am complete in Christ?"

How does being complete in Christ affect the following areas of my life?

- My marriage?
    o Do I place unrealistic expectations on my husband to keep me feeling complete?
    o How can my completeness in Christ allow me to love him freely without expecting anything in return?
- My children's life?
    o Do I look to them for fulfillment?
    o What happens when they grow up and leave home?
    o Can I be complete in an empty nest?
- My career?
    o Will money buy what I am looking for and make me whole?
    o Is my security in my job rather than in Christ?

- My community and friends?
    - o Is my significance attached to the positions I hold in my church or society?
    - o Is my significance attached to my husband's military rank?

Bless you, wives of warriors, for your diligence this week. I'm excited about the rest of this study and how God will work through other Biblical Principles we will learn to apply to our lives. Our lives will change and we will act differently. To Him be the glory for ever and ever. Amen!

Week Two

The Gift Of Grace

> *"By the grace of God I am what I am and His grace to me was not without effect."*
>
> 1 CORINTHIANS 15:10

*I*f there has been one question people have asked me over and over again in the many years that I have used a wheelchair for mobility, it is, "Ronda, how do you do it? How do you go throughout your entire day using a wheelchair for mobility? Everything you do is so hard, yet you make it look so easy. How do you do this?"

Always ready to respond in such a manner that will bring glory to God, I quote the apostle Paul in 1 Corinthians 15:10, "By the grace of God I am what I am and His grace to me was not without effect."

This week we are going to take a close look at God's gift of grace. Grace is what enables us to be complete in Him. Grace is what enables us to live our lives according to God's will, regardless of our circumstances. Grace enables us to reach peaks we thought were unreachable; to overcome valleys we thought were unconquerable and to remain strong and steadfast in our faith.

We hear the word spoken many times with so many different meanings. There is a plethora of songs, poems, books and devotions on the subject of grace, all of which try to convey to the listener or reader the wonder of it all.

Consider this another vain attempt to humanly explain one of the greatest mysteries of mankind—Why did God choose us, amidst our imperfections and weaknesses, to be the vessels and instruments by which He fills the whole earth with the knowledge of His glory?

There are many different aspects of grace. Grace is like a diamond in that there is only one stone but many different facets. This week we are going to study the various facets or workings of grace in our lives. We will study Prevenient Grace, Saving Grace, Sanctifying Grace, Sustaining Grace and Restorative Grace, all which ultimately come from the one and only Spirit of Grace. (Hebrews 10:29)

I pray you will enjoy our study this week as we focus on this wonderful thing called grace. The more we learn about it, the more we see it truly is amazing!

DAY ONE: PRAISE

For today's praise and worship, let's interactively read one of the devotional Psalms. These are the Psalms that contain precious and personal promises to us from God. These Psalms usually start by reminding the people of Israel what God has done for them in the past and end by acknowledging trust in God's unfailing love to provide for their needs for the future.

These psalms declare the mighty works of God, they declare God as Maker and Master of the entire universe who delights greatly in blessing those who put their trust in Him. They declare God as compassionate, good and kind, slow to anger and abounding in love. Oh, the grace God pours out in abundance to those who call upon His name!

Today, let's rejoice in the wonderful things the Lord has done as we read Psalm 147. As you read, meditate on every word, every prayer and every promise. Praise Him with your whole heart, your whole mind and your whole being!

1.   <u>Read Psalm 147 interactively</u>

  • How does this Psalm declare God as Maker and Master over all?
  • List the promises God makes for those who trust in Him.
  • How do these promises apply to your life right now?
  • What makes God happy?
  • How does God reveal himself to us?

God promises to sustain, satisfy and supply all our needs!! He heals the brokenhearted and binds up their wound, grants us peace and protection. What a wonderful God we serve!!

Continue to meditate on these assurances throughout the day. Tomorrow we will get into the meat of our lesson, the Gift of Grace. I think we are off to a very good start, don't you?

DAY TWO: THE PRINCIPLE

The Biblical Principle for this week is: '*By the grace of God, I am who I am.*'

1.   <u>Read 1 Corinthians 15:10</u>
2.   <u>Read John 1:14,16,17; Romans 5:21; 1 Cor. 1:4; 2 Timothy 1:9</u>

  • With whom is grace directly connected?

Ultimately, New Testament grace comes in the person of Jesus Christ and is directly associated with Him. The apostle John declared Jesus came from the Father and was full of grace and truth. Through Him grace and truth come. Paul tells us grace was given to us in Jesus Christ. Grace reigns in the righteousness that is ours through Jesus Christ leading us to eternal life.

In order to understand grace more fully, we must understand its Biblical definition. The English definition of grace usually refers to a personal characteristic of polished elegance, where as the Biblical definition of the word grace is far different.

In the New Testament the Greek word is *'charis'* and means *"of the merciful kindness by which God, exerting his holy influence upon souls, turns them to Christ, keeps, strengthens, increases them in Christian faith, knowledge, affection, and kindles them to the exercise of the Christian virtues."* (Strong)

In other words, grace is the means through which the Holy Spirit dispenses his merciful kindness to the whole human race.

For a Biblical example of this principle of God's grace, let's look at the parable of the workers in the vineyard. I know this parable is chockfull of symbolism, referring to God and the salvation of believers. But just this once, let's look at this parable in literal terms. Let's put ourselves in the place of the eleventh hour workers and view this parable from their perspective

3. Read Matthew 20:1–15

    •   Why do you think the Landowner asked the people to work in his fields?

    •   As the day wore on, who had the greater need? The workers or the Landowner?

    •   How do you think the eleventh hours workers felt when they were paid a full days wages?

    •   Did the Landowner pay them according to what they earned or did he pay them according to what they needed?

Jerry Bridges, author of Transforming Grace, explains this parable from the workers perspective in the context of the culture at that time. I have taken the liberty to paraphrase and condense this information.

It was customary in those days for the workers of the fields to stand around the marketplace until they were hired to work in a field. They were paid at the end of each day and usually spent their money on food to feed their family. If they did not work at all during the day, their family would have to go without something to eat.

As the day wore on the landowner kept observing more and more people standing around the marketplace. No one had hired them to work. Doing them a favor by giving them the opportunity to earn money to feed their family, he told them to go work in his fields.

Most of the working day had passed. There was only one hour left when the landowner noticed people still standing around. When he asked them why they were not working they replied, 'because no one has hired us.' Imagine the desperation they must have felt as the day wore on and no one had asked them to work. They would not have any money to buy food for their family.

Again, giving them an opportunity to earn money that would buy food for their family, he told them to go work in his field. Relieved to have even an hour's worth of work, they eagerly went off into the fields. It would not be much, but at least they would have a little something to buy some food for their wives and children.

When it came time to pay the workers, the ones who started last were not only paid first, they were paid a full day's wages for only an hour's worth of work! Imagine the excitement and joy those eleventh hour workers must have felt. They expected to receive an hour's worth of pay for an hour's worth of work, but instead, they received a full day's pay.

The same principle applies to people in the Kingdom of God. The fact is we are all eleventh hour workers when it comes to God's grace. God gives his merciful kindness to each one of us, instead of what we deserve. He gives his blessings according to the riches of His grace, not out of debt. We all deserve so little, yet He gives us so much; more than we will ever comprehend or realize this side of eternity. Dependant not upon that which we have done for God, grace is all about what God has done for us.

This finishes our lesson for today. Meditate on God's grace and thank Him for it. It really is amazing!

Day Three and Four: Proof Of The Principle

We learned from our previous lesson that grace is the means by which God gives us his merciful kindness. It is the means by which He keeps and strengthens us. We learned God gives his grace through the person of Jesus Christ. He gives his grace according to his riches, not according to our debt, and that God is generous in his outpouring of it. Today we are going to look at the various aspects of grace and how the Spirit of Grace works in our life.

Prevenient Grace: The means by which we are called to faith and repentance.

1. <u>Read John 6:44,45 & 65; Galatians 1:13–16; 1 Corinthians 1:9</u>

Act. 10:23-34

- Who initiates our coming to God?

- Who calls us into His fellowship?

- How was Paul called by God?

- Think about the time before you came to know God. What led up to that point? What were you going through at the time?

- As you look back on your life, can you see God's prevenient grace at work?

God initiates our coming to him by his prevenient grace. It is His holy influence and relentless pursuit of our souls that causes us to turn to Him. It is prevenient grace that alone facilitates repentance and faith. Through prevenient grace, God works in our lives to bring us unto Himself, even before most of us realize it!

We cannot appreciate the gift of salvation until we recognize our need for a Savior. No one sees this need and seeks God on their own. (Romans 3:11) Prevenient grace leads us to see ourselves as a sinner in need of a Savior; completely helpless, in need of a Helper; and as lost, in need of a Lord.

Prevenient grace is also what keeps us in God's care and protection. My husband and son both grew up knowing God, therefore, they have no profound 'coming to Jesus' salvation story. A friend's daughter in a similar situation feels she has no 'real' testimony to tell her friends about how she came to know the Lord. "There is nothing too exciting about someone who has known God all her life," she has often remarked.

To people such as this, the truth is they have the most exciting testimony of all!! God's prevenient grace kept them from making lifestyle choices that could easily lead to undesirable consequences. His grace kept them from experiencing the dangers of the secular teenage lifestyle. Consequently, I call my husband, son and others who have been kept by God since childhood, "trophies" of God's prevenient grace! Oh, the wonder of it all!

Let's look now at the next stage, Saving Grace.

Saving Grace: The means by which we are saved from our past sins and brought into fellowship with God.

This is the most familiar work of grace. Prevenient grace brings us to the point of repentance and faith, but it is saving grace that actually spares us from God's wrath and allows us to come into the wonder-filled presence of God. We have been saved from a negative situation to a new life, a new hope and new interests.

2. Read Ephesians 2:8

    • Does our salvation come from anything we have done?

3. Read Colossians 1:21,22; Romans 3:20–24; Ephesians 2:1–5

    • Notice the word "BUT" in these verses. Read them again and contrast what we have been saved from and meditate on that which we have been saved to.

Our spiritual position changes from being separated from God to being brought into His Kingdom. An exchange has taken place. There is an exchange of something worthless for something beautiful, something wanting for something blessed. Oh, the wonder of saving grace!

God's prevenient grace leads us to his saving grace. Once we have received his saving grace, we then begin to experience his Sanctifying Grace.

Sanctifying Grace: The means by which we are transformed into His likeness in order that our lives will bring him greater glory.

God has one goal in mind for believers: to fill the earth with the knowledge and glory of God. In order to do that however, God must first mold us into vessels He can use to accomplish His purposes. God does not save us and then leave us to wander around like lost puppies. He begins immediately to work in our life to transform us into His image. I'm reminded of the subtitle of Max Lucado's book, Just Like Jesus: "God loves us just the way we are, but He refuses to let us stay that way."

4. Read Philippians 1:6
5. Read 1 Corinthians 1:2

- What have we been in Jesus Christ?

- Is this action past, present or future?

- To what are we being called?

- Is this action past, present or future?

Notice, that we *have been* sanctified in Jesus Christ. This verb tense implies a past action. When we come to know Christ, our spiritual position changes forever. "We are made holy by virtue of our relationship with Jesus Christ." (KJ Study Bible) As we see from studying saving grace, we go from being apart from God to being reconciled unto him throughout eternity.

Now that we have a new position, the Holy Spirit leads us to new actions. We are called to be holy, to be set apart, to be blameless. The verb used here implies a present tense. We must learn to take off the old self and put on the new self. (Colossians 3:9) We do this by giving God our old hearts, and letting Him give us a new one.

The heart patient must give up his old, diseased heart before the heart surgeon can put in the new, healthy one. There is only room for one heart. The patient must ultimately decide which heart he wants, but it is the surgeon who does the transplant. So it is with God. God does the work within our hearts, but we must be willing to allow him to do it!

Most of the time God gives us new hearts through Bible study, prayer, church attendance and fellowship with other believers. These are all means through which God uses to sanctify us.

However, sometimes our new hearts require a more rigorous workout. These workouts cannot take place in the comfort of a home Bible study or the warmth of a church sanctuary. These workouts can only be experienced through the hardships and difficulties of life. This is what I call Spiritual Boot Camp and is the most misunderstood work of grace.

6.   Read 1 Peter 1:6,7; Malachi 3:2–4; Isaiah 1:25

- What is the purpose of the testing of our faith?
- What does God hope to remove from us?
- What value can we place on strengthening our faith and refining our character?

Faith is not faith until it is tested!! We usually do not like to be in circumstances where this happens. They are painful, uncomfortable, and oftentimes, unrelenting. It's quite natural for us to try to escape these times of testing, but it is clearly God's will for us to experience strengthening and refinement during Spiritual Boot Camp at some point in our lives.

You must always remember *God wants to use us, not abuse us!* He wants to make our new hearts strong. This may involve making a few changes in us as God removes our impurities and purges away our imperfections.

In the process of our refinement, I wish I could tell you God uses cotton balls and cotton swabs as His instruments. But I would be telling you a lie. Just as the sculptor must use sharp tools to transform a plain block of wood into a beautiful piece of art, so must our Sculptor use sharp tools on us from time to time. Purifying fire is VERY HOT!

• We must change the way we think about trials and hardships and begin to see them as a means of God's sanctifying grace. He is working in our lives to make us more like Him. He is working in our lives so that we can work more effectively for Him. Once we start thinking differently about this process called sanctification, we will start acting differently.

I'm so convinced God allows difficult circumstances in our life so we will learn to depend on Him. As much as we tend to resist this work of grace, it is impossible to experience His sustaining grace without it! This leads us to the next aspect of grace: Sustaining Grace.

Sustaining Grace: The means by which we are sustained during difficult times.

7. <u>Read Psalm 9:10; 55:22; 146:9; Isaiah 46:3,4; 1 Corinthians 1:8,9; 2 Corinthians 12:9</u>

[handwritten: I Sa. 18:14; I Sa. 20:41-21:9a]

- What is the promise of these verses?
- Since when has God known us?
- How long does He promise to be with us?
- What is sufficient for us in our weakness?
- What does God promise to do for us during these times?

God promises to always be with us. He has known us since we were conceived. He promises to keep us strong to the end when all our hairs are gray. He promises His protection and His presence. He promises to keep us safely tucked up under His wings. Wives of our warriors can live confidently in Christ through extended duty deployments because of God's sustaining grace!

One of my favorite Biblical illustrations of God's sustaining grace is from the life of David.

8. <u>Read 1 Samuel 20:41–21:9</u>

- Why did David weep more than Jonathan?
- To whom did David first run in his time of desperation?
- What two items did the priest give David?

As we jump into David's life at this point, David realizes he is about to lose everything and everybody he loves. His wife, his family, and his friends all had to be forsaken in order to run away from the deadly pursuit of King Saul. David had just convinced his best friend Jonathan that Saul was indeed trying to kill him and that he must run for his life. As they hugged and embraced good-bye, David was overtaken with grief and indeed, wept more.

Notice the first person David ran to was the priest. He ran directly to Ahimelech, perhaps to seek the Lord's guidance. If we expect God to sustain us during our difficult times, we must run to him right away! Admittedly, we begin to see a few character flaws in David as he resorts to lying to the priest upon his arrival. Unfortunately, Ahimelech is later killed as a result of this meeting. But we must not miss the point that David ran to God first.

When David asked if he had anything to eat, Ahimelech gave him only what he had: leftover consecrated bread. This was the bread that was placed in the Holy place of the tabernacle that represented God's presence. As Ahimelech gave this bread to David, I believe God was assuring David of His presence in his life at that time, as well as promising His presence during the next fifteen years as David fled in exile.

The only weapon Ahimelech had to give David was the very sword David used to slay Goliath, the giant. A coincidence? I don't think so. I believe God was also promising David his protection during the difficult years to come.

We learn a great deal about God's sustaining grace from this illustration. When we run to God in the midst of difficulty He promises His presence and protection. There will be times in our lives when our circumstances seem to be in direct conflict of this promise, but we must accept it by faith. Just as David constantly trusted in God's unfailing love, so must we. Eventually, David was restored as the King of Israel. We too, will eventually be restored as we trust in God's unfailing love and grace to sustain us during difficult times.

If you are in a position where you are questioning God's presence and sustaining grace in your life, ask Him to reveal himself to you. It may be in the form of a phone call from a friend, a card, a letter, or just noticing a perfectly formed flower and realizing the God who made that flower also made you! And you are so much more important to Him than that flower.

God sustains His children, no matter where He leads them. And after He sustains us, He always restores us.

Restorative Grace: The means by which we are restored and made strong once again.

9. Read 1 Peter 5:10; Ephesians 3:20; Job 42:10–17; Ruth 4:13–17

    • How is God described in 1 Peter 5:10?

    • What three things will He do for us?

    • How much more does He do for us?

    • How were both Ruth and Job restored?

God is in the restoration business! After you have suffered a little while He will restore you! David was restored as the King of Israel. In the end Job was given much more than what he originally possessed. And Naomi was given her long sought after son. God restored them, making them once again strong, firm and steadfast.

Ephesians 3:20 (my favorite verse!) tells us God does immeasurably more than all we can ask or ever imagine, according to His power working inside us! God blesses us beyond measure when we trust in His unfailing love.

However, I want us to consider another form of restoration: emotional and spiritual restoration. God will not always restore us in the form of physical or material blessings. Sometimes He makes us strong and steadfast in our faith without changing our circumstances.

10. Read Habakkuk 3:17–19

    • Describe the physical circumstances of this writer.

    • How does he describe his relationship with God?

    • Is his joy and strength in God dependent upon his circumstances?

    • In spite of difficult circumstances, how is Habakkuk restored?

    • Is it possible to have restoration without a change of circumstances?

God may not always change your circumstances, but He will change your heart.

Barring a miracle from God, I will never walk again. I have not been able to stand up and walk for 30 years. No matter how long God allows me to live on this earth, I will have spent most of my life using a wheelchair for mobility.

Yet, I consider myself restored. God makes me strong, firm and steadfast in my faith. I agree with Paul who wrote in Philippians 3:7, "But whatever was to my profit I now consider loss for the sake of Christ." Knowing Christ spiritually is much more important to me than the physical act of walking.

As your relationship with the Savior deepens, His restorative grace will make you strong, firm and steadfast, perfect and complete, lacking in nothing. Sound familiar? (The principle from our last lesson!) That is exactly what He wants us to be!

I know we have had many Scriptures to look up and wrestle with for the past two days. I pray God has spoken to you in a fresh, new way to help you understand more fully the wonderful thing called grace. All of us are touched by each aspect of His grace at some point in our lives. Ultimately, like Paul, we are who we are because of God's grace.

Tomorrow, we will learn how to recognize this wonderful thing called grace and how God is working in our lives through it.

DAY FIVE: PRAISE AND PRACTICUM

This week we studied the principle: *'By the Grace of God I am who I am.'* We studied the various aspects of grace and how God uses it in our lives.

For our interactive praise and worship today, let's read Psalm 103. This is another devotional Psalm in which David praises God to his fullest. He praises God for His works and His ways; he praises God for His wonders; and he praises God for His word, all given to us simply out of His glorious grace!

1. <u>Read Psalm 103 interactively</u>

   - What benefits does the Psalmist speak of in vs. 1–5?
   - According to this weeks' lesson, do we deserve any of those benefits?
   - Why does God give us these benefits? (vs. 8)
   - How great is His love towards us?
   - How long will His love last?
   - How do these promises affect your life today?

For our practicum today, spend the next few moments reflecting upon the following questions:

   - How was God's prevenient grace demonstrated in my life?
   - Am I fully aware of the truth of His saving grace?
   - What is my reaction as I realize where I stood spiritually before I came to Christ?
   - How has God's sanctifying grace been at work in my life?
   - Can I look back and see my growth as a Christian?
   - Am I experiencing some hardships now that may be attributed to God's sanctifying grace?
   - List the ways He has sustained you during difficult times in the past.
   - How did He restore you?

Isn't God's grace amazing?

This concludes our study for the week. Through God's grace, He knows us intimately and gives us everything we need to live an abundant life, right here, right now. He does not pay us according to our iniquities, but rather according to the riches of His glorious grace.

Continue to dwell on this wonderful truth. Pay attention to how God is working in your life to make you more like Him. God wants to use us, not abuse us!! His grace keeps us and strengthens us. Like Paul, we can all echo the words, "But by the grace of God, I am what I am, and his grace to me was not without effect." (1 Corinthians 15:10)

As wives of warriors, when we realize God's grace sanctifies us with each and every move, sustains us while our husbands are away, and restores and strengthens us once we have relocated to our new assignment, we *can* unpack those boxes one more time, finding excitement in placing our pictures on yet another wall.

Now that's a gift we want to accept!

Week Three

Moving: A Missionary Journey

"But our citizenship is in Heaven. And we eagerly await a Savior from there, the Lord Jesus Christ."

Philippians 3:20

In a recent conversation with a new friend from our PWOC, I learned she and her family moved three times in the last four years!

"What an opportunity for the Lord to show His faithfulness," was my reply.

"Oh," she said. "That's a good way to look at it!"

In this chapter we will discuss a very important topic for those of us in military service: *moving!!!* Long ago I encouraged my friends to enter my address into their address books in pencil, knowing it would change in just a few, short years. I'm sure by now the little box that holds the Sturgill's address is worn thin from the constant erasing. There may even be a hole in the paper that once held our place of residence!

All joking aside, moving involves much more than simply changing an address in an address book; it's a complete change of everything familiar to us. Change is something most of us don't like. No matter how beneficial a change may be for us, most of us register change as loss. In the case of a military move, we definitely perceive this as a loss: the loss of friends, the loss of a supportive church, the loss of our children's schools and activities, the loss of a friendly familiarity with our community and neighborhoods.

But we also see moving as a unique opportunity: an opportunity to encounter new experiences, an opportunity to make new friends, an opportunity to live in different parts of the world and to discover everything our new location has to offer. (For me this usually means finding a great restaurant!). We are excited about finding a new house and turning it into a home, planting flowers and getting to know our neighbors.

In this lesson, we will discover the importance God has placed on moving His people in order to achieve His ultimate goal: to fill the earth with the knowledge of the glory of God. As we will see from the very beginning of time, God never intended for His people to remain in our comfortable 'Holy Huddle.' His purposes were achieved only when He found servants who were willing to 'go and make disciples of all nations.' (Matthew 28:19)

So let's begin our study. As we draw comparisons of how God worked in the past and how He works today, may we find a renewed excitement about moving and the unique opportunities it presents us.

DAY ONE: PRAISE

In our ever-changing military environment, we must know for sure we have a God, steady and secure on which to stand. Today we will focus on Scriptures that reveal God as our Rock, God as our Refuge, and God as our ever-present resting place.

1. Interactively read and meditate upon the following verses:

   - 2 Samuel 22:2
   - Psalm 18:2
   - Psalm 92:15
   - Deuteronomy 32:3,4

What does the phrase, "God is my rock" mean to you?

2.   <u>Interactively read and meditate upon these verses:</u>

   - Psalm 5:11
   - Psalm 9:9
   - Psalm 31:2
   - Nahum 1:7

What does the phrase, "God is my refuge" mean to you?

3.   <u>Interactively read and meditate upon these verses:</u>

   - Psalm 62:1
   - Psalm 91:1
   - Jeremiah 6:16
   - Matthew 11:28

What does the phrase, "My soul finds rest in God alone" mean to you?

Ladies, let us rejoice we have a God who is our Rock, our Refuge, and our Resting place!

DAY TWO: THE PRINCIPLE

The Biblical principle we are going to study this week is: *'Our purpose as believers is to fill the earth with the knowledge of the glory of God.'*

This principle is actually very exciting, especially when you consider how perfectly our military lifestyle is suited for such purposes. From the very beginning God's ultimate goal for His people has simply been to fill the earth with the knowledge of the glory of God.

1. Read the following verses:

    - Numbers 14:21
    - Habakkuk 2:14
    - Isaiah 6:3; 11:9; 43:7
    - What is the theme of these verses?
    - What is God's goal for His people?
    - Why did He create us?

We can see clearly God desires to use us to fill the earth with the knowledge of the glory of God. Next, we are going to look at how He accomplishes this goal.

2. Read Genesis 11:1–9

    - What were the people trying to do?
    - How willing were they to be separated from their family and friends?
    - What happened after God confused their language?
    - What was the purpose of God scattering the people?

What we see here is really no different than what we see today: people would much rather stick together where it is comfortable than to be scattered all over the world, far away from friends and family. God had already begun His plan to use people to accomplishes His purposes!

3. Read Genesis 12:1–5

    - What did God tell Abraham to do?
    - Who was he supposed to leave?
    - What was Abraham's response?
    - Notice what he took with him? Now that was some PCS!!!

4. Read Hebrews 11:8–10

    •   How was Abraham able to pack up everything and move?

    •   What did Abraham consider his real home?

    •   How does the writer of Hebrews define Abraham's idea of living on earth?

Abraham was able to pack up his household goods and move because of his faith in God. He knew God was able to do all that He promised. God was his rock, his refuge, and his resting place. But more importantly, Abraham grasped a truth we would all be wise to hold on to as we move around from one duty station to another: his real home is not here on earth at all, but in heaven with his Heavenly Father. Oh, that we would remember that as the packers make their way through the house for the hundredth time!

Let's read one more verse.

5. Read Matthew 8:20

    •   What did Jesus say about His home?

Here we have the first example of the Gospel being spread through a mobile ministry. We see God spreading His word and His light. He is spreading the knowledge of the glory of God by means of a pair of sandals and a walking stick. Jesus moved around constantly from one place to another, never calling anywhere home. He simply went where God led him, desiring God's will to be done in his life instead of his own. What an example we have!

This will bring today's lesson to a close. Praise God for all He is teaching you concerning His purpose for your life and how He will accomplish that purpose!

DAY THREE AND FOUR: PROOF OF THE PRINCIPLE

Today we are going to take a closer look at the ministry of Paul. We are going to join him as he prepared for his first missionary journey as well as tag along on his second. Clearly, the Gospel is spread by moving people from one place to another! Without the mobility factor written into the picture, God's plan to fill the earth with the knowledge of His glory would had to have been accomplished by some other means.

Our transient military lifestyle is a perfect vehicle for God to use to spread the Gospel to people around the world. As we study Paul's missionary journeys we will notice similarities between his assignments and ours.

I can hear all of the mothers saying right now, "But it was easy for Paul, he did not have any kids to move around with him!" It's true he did not have any kids in tow as he PCS'd from one coastal town of the Mediterranean to another. However, I'm a firm believer that our children's reaction to our moves is cued from our reaction. If we see each new assignment as an opportunity for positive change, I believe our children will feel the same way.

Let's move on to our study!

1. <u>Read Acts 11:19–26; Acts 13:2–4</u>

- What do these verses say about the church in Antioch?
- How long did Barnabas and Paul minister in Antioch?
- Was this a vibrant, growing church?
- What were the disciples called for the first time?
- How did the church send them off on their journey?

Antioch was a vibrant, growing church and became the home church of Barnabas and Paul. It is from here Paul begins his three missionary journeys. Although excited about the work to which God called him, it must have been hard to leave behind such a loving, caring church, located in an area with which he was completely familiar. They left simply by faith, being led by the Holy Spirit.

As people leave our chapel community, we often send them off to their next duty assignment in the same manner as did the church in Antioch with Barnabas and Paul. We pray for them and committ them to God's grace. I'm especially touched by the farewell scene as Paul departed the church in Ephesus. Acts 20:37 tells that the people wept as they embraced him and kissed him. What grieved them the most was that they would never see him again.

Just like us when we move, we often leave behind a loving, caring body of believers with whom we have developed deep friendships. For me, leaving those precious friends behind is by far the most difficult aspect of moving. My heart has been broken in two more times than I care to mention over leaving prayer partners and spiritual mentors.

I want to point out that Paul never worked alone on his missionary journeys—he always had co-workers; partners in the faith who helped and encouraged him. We too, are given co-workers as we labor in the fields. At most military bases there are Chapels in which to worship. The Protestant Women of the Chapel (PWOC) are our co-laborers for Christ. It has been my experience as I leave behind my co-laborers at one base, God always provides co-laborers at another. God weaves our lives together and puts in our path the very people who will join us in our work.

2.   Read Acts 14:26–28

- To where did Barnabas and Paul return?
- What was the first item of business they took care of when they returned home?

Oh, how we love to report the wonderful things God does for us! Barnabas and Paul were so excited about telling their fellow believers all God did for them and how He opened many doors, they reported this as soon as they arrived.

Although some of us have the wonderful opportunity to go back to a base where we have previously served, most of us do not. However, we do make friends with whom we keep in touch for years to come. And of what do our correspondences usually consist?

We report to each other all the wonderful things God has done in our lives and in the lives of our loved ones. My e:mails are filled with reports of what God is doing at the base we are serving. I get so excited when I see Him work in the lives of the people with whom we are involved. I report on the Bible studies I lead as well as the Bible studies I take. I report on what is happening in our PWOC, I report on what God is doing in the lives of my son and husband. Yes, Christians enjoy reporting good news!!!

Now, let's tag along with Paul on his second missionary journey.

3. <u>Read Acts 15:36</u>

    • Who does Paul want to go back and check on?

Paul wants to go back and check on the churches he and Barnabas started on their first missionary journey. Barnabas quickly agrees; however, at this point he and Paul go different directions with different co-workers.

Let's join Paul and Silas on their journey.

4. <u>Read Acts 16:6–10; Proverbs 16:9,19:21; Isaiah 46:10; Jeremiah 10:23</u>

    • Who was clearly in control of their journey?

    • How was this evidenced?

    • What was Paul's response?

    • Do you think Paul had a plan when they started out?

    • Whose plan prevailed?

Does this sound familiar to our military assignments? Although this has never happened to us, I know of people who were packed up and ready to leave for one location, when they were redirected in mid stream to another. God always reserves the right to redirect his people. Sometimes He just does not want us to go to a particular assignment at that time. I'm aware of one Chaplain who finally received an assignment he wanted after three tries.

I don't know how the system works in the other branches of service concerning the assignment system, but in the Air Force, the members are required to complete a 'dream sheet.' A 'dream sheet' is a list of preferred locations where you would like to serve for your next duty assignment.

After prayerfully and carefully filling out this form, the Air Force usually sends you to the location where you are most needed. In our sixteen years of military service, we have received our first choice of assignments once!

However, it is perfectly clear every location and duty assignment has been exactly where God wanted us to go. From the very beginning we have believed the same God who created the universe is also the God of the military assignment system. God is large and in charge and each assignment is hand-picked especially by Him. It may not be where we originally planned to go, but it is clearly where God intended to send us in order to accomplish His purpose for our life.

God was also in charge of Paul's itinerary. Notice how quickly Paul abandoned his plan and obeyed the leading of the Holy Spirit. As a result God's purpose was accomplished. Let's see exactly what that was.

5. Read Acts 16:11–34

- Describe what happened to Lydia?
- Describe what happened to Paul and Silas while they were in prison?
- After reading vs. 22–24, what do you think may have been going through their minds?
- Do you think they may have questioned the Lord's redirecting them?
- What were they doing before the earthquake?
- What was the result of Paul and Silas's trust and faith in God during this difficult assignment?

The fact that Paul and Silas experienced such hardship during this assignment reminds me that not all of our duty assignments are pleasant. Our children may be having trouble in school, we may be having a difficult time finding a job, our husband could be under an enormous amount of stress in his job, or he may be often deployed, leaving us home alone to keep the fires burning.

At one time or another we've all had an assignment that has prompted us to ask the question, "Why did God ever send us here?" Nothing seems to be working out as we had planned. Where Paul and Silas were physically in prison, our lack of faith and trust in God puts us there emotionally.

What were Paul and Silas doing before the earthquake came? They were praying and singing hymns! After experiencing humiliation, shame, physical torture and confinement, they were praising and worshipping God!

Oh, the lessons we can learn from this example! As hard as we may think our assignments are, we would be hard pressed to say they compared to the experience here of Paul and Silas. As they praised and worshipped God in the midst of their hardship, God was at work to fill the earth with the knowledge of the glory of God. An earthquake came, the prisoners were set free and many people came to know and accept the Gospel. If we allow God to use us in the same manner during our difficult assignments, who knows who may come to be a believer?

We must believe firmly each duty assignment is hand picked for us by a loving, compassionate God. When we look for God at each assignment we will find him. When we yield ourselves and surrender to Him, He is able to accomplish His purpose in and through our lives, making each assignment truly a missionary journey!!

DAY FIVE: PRAISE AND PRACTICUM

Before we begin our praise and practicum let's review what we have studied so far this week.

Our purpose as believers is to fill the earth with the knowledge of the glory of God. God accomplishes this goal by literally moving people around the world. Since military service is a very transient lifestyle, it is very conducive to putting this principle into practice.

God is God of the assignment system. Although most assignments are very pleasant in nature, occasionally we do get one we would not have chosen for ourselves. If we can learn to submit to His leading and yield ourselves to His will for our lives, we are bound to see exciting things happen in our lives and in the lives of those people around us.

Today we are going to apply this principle to our own lives. First, let's begin with a time of praise and worship. As with before, please read these Scriptures interactively!

1. <u>Read Psalm 93; Psalm 103:19</u>

    - What is the theme of these verses?
    - Who is on the throne?
    - Who is on the throne in your life?

2. <u>Read Isaiah 55:8–11</u>

    - How do our thoughts and ways compare with God's?
    - What does this say about the purposes of God?
    - Is there an area in your life where you may be questioning how God is working?

Think back over your past duty assignments and answer the following questions:

- How often have you moved in your years of military service?
- Were you ever given assignments of your choice?
- How has God been faithful to meet your needs in your previous assignments? Be specific.
- What are you trusting Him for in this present assignment?
- Are you allowing Him to work in and through you to fill the earth with the knowledge of the glory of God?

Ladies, this concludes our study for this week. I hope you are encouraged in your walk with God after having studied parts of Paul's missionary journeys. The God who worked in Paul's life is the same God who works in ours. Although our circumstances may be different than Paul's, the Biblical principles of how God works are still the same.

May you rejoice in each new assignment as being Spirit led and hand-picked from God and may He bless you immensely as you continue your service to God and your country through your missionary journeys!

Week Four

Working Through Our Weakness

"I can do everything through Him who gives me strength."
Philippians 4:13

When my husband and I were thinking of starting our family twenty years ago, I did a lot of research on pregnancies of other women who are also paraplegics. I read everything I could get my hands on that chronicled their experiences and whether or not they had healthy, normal babies.

Was it hard to function from a wheelchair being 20–30 pounds heavier? Was it hard to take off the weight that normally is left after a pregnancy? Did the baby develop properly in the uterus, being 'squished' all the time from sitting down? Oh, the questions were endless as I focused primarily on the physiology of the pregnancy.

I soon found out first hand what it was like for a paraplegic to be pregnant: very normal. Finally, it was time for the delivery. As with every pregnancy, nothing really prepares you for feeling like your insides are on fire and you are being slowly ripped apart! But after many hours of huffing and puffing exactly like I was taught, Toby was finally born. As I looked at the red, white and wriggly creature the doctor placed on my belly, I was quite shocked.

"Oh my," I said out loud. "That's a big baby!"

"Oh my," I thought to myself. "Now what do I do?"

I was very nervous as I dressed Toby to take him home from the hospital. He was lying in my lap, a perfect fit with his head on my knees and his feet up against my belly. I turned my wheelchair to go to the other side of the room when much to my horror, my wheelchair went one way and he went another. Thankfully I have quick reflexes and I reached down and grabbed him before he fell on the floor head first.

"Oh my," I thought. "I've already dropped him and I have not even left the hospital yet!" For fear of not being allowed to take him home, I did not report this incident to the rest of my family!

Upon arriving home, my mother carried Toby into the house and placed him in his cradle. Sleeping very soundly, he really was a cute little baby. However, part of me wished he would wake up eighteen years later. Suddenly the thought of taking care of my son while using a wheelchair for mobility completely overwhelmed me.

"What was I thinking having this baby?" I thought.

Instead of sleeping for the next eighteen years, he only slept for the next eighteen minutes. As he began to wriggle and cry, I realized I had to pick him up out of his cradle.

"How am I going to do this?" I wondered.

Just as I thought, I bent over to pick him up, lost my balance and fell right into the cradle with him! That did it!

"I can't do this," I cried, bursting into tears. "This is all a mistake. I should never have had this baby."

At that point my mother grabbed my shoulders, bent down and looked me square in the eye.

"Oh yes you can do this," she firmly responded. "You will learn to take care of this baby the same way you have learned to do everything else since your accident. This baby is no mistake. He is a gift from God."

"Well then," I thought, "God is going to have to help me take care of him!"

You know what? God did exactly that. My son is now twenty years old, has a heart for God and serves Him on a praise and worship team. However, each stage of his development found me just as overwhelmed as I was the first day I brought him home from the hospital.

As I continually cried out to God for help, God worked in amazing ways to help me care for my son. He worked through my weakness and enabled me to do all the 'mom' things moms do with their children. I found out that we really can do all things through Him who gives us strength!

This week our lesson will focus on God as He continually proves Himself faithful in the lives of those who trust Him, especially when confronted with our weaknesses.

Wives of our warriors are all too familiar with seemingly insurmountable situations in which we feel extremely weak. No sooner then when our husbands step out the door for a 90-day TDY, every electrical gadget we own goes on the blink! The water pipes break, the car battery dies and one of the kids gets sick . . . all at the same time!

At one time or another each one of us experiences the helpless feeling of not having enough hands, feet, time and energy to do everything that needs to be done. We are happily married yet suddenly, we find ourselves a single parent, juggling a schedule that tests the organizational skills of the most proficient type A personality!

"I can't do this," we cry out loudly to God, wondering if He hears our prayers. "I'm not cut out to be a military wife. Either I've married the wrong man, or You have called him into the wrong career."

I often imagine God up in Heaven gently smiling as He whispers His reply to our pleas, "I know you cannot do all of this by yourself. But I can do the work through you, if you will only give me the chance. And no, you did not marry the wrong man. You are a couple, one in the same, a team, lifetime partners. If I have called your husband to military service, I have also called you. I will supply all your needs according to my glorious riches."

This week we are going to focus on Scriptures that explain how God supplies all of our needs and how He enables us to overcome our weaknesses and the obstacles we often face. We will look at examples from people in the past to see how God equipped them for His service. We will learn how to apply the same principles to our lives today, being confident God gives us everything we need to accomplish the work He has called us to do.

Let's begin our study with a time of Praise and Worship!

DAY ONE: PRAISE

1. <u>Read Psalm 145 interactively</u>

    *   How often does the Psalmist praise God?
    *   How are the works of God known through time?
    *   In verses 3–7, how are the works of God described?
    *   What are the attributes of God that are mentioned in this Psalm?
    *   Where is the Lord when His people call on Him?
    *   After studying this Psalm, has your perception of God's presence changed?

Aren't the attributes of God listed in this Psalm wonderful? Faithful to all His promises; good, loving and compassionate towards all He has made. Did He make you? Then He is good, loving and compassionate towards you.

He fulfills the desires of those who fear Him. Do you fear God? Then He promises to fulfill your desires. The Lord is near to all who call on Him. Do you call on Him? Then He is near. His works are mighty, glorious, awesome and great. They tell of the glory of His kingdom and speak of His splendor. By them we know He is God and there is no other.

For the rest of the week we will look at His awesome and mighty works in the lives of several people throughout the Bible. We will draw some comparisons of each life and see a thread of consistency of how God works to accomplish His will. Then we will apply these same principles to our lives.

Just as God was faithful to do awesome and mighty acts in the lives of those who have gone before, we can trust Him to do the same in ours. For His sake and for His glory, He WANTS to work through our weakness, He WANTS us to live victoriously, and He WANTS to fulfill our desires.

Read the last verse of Psalm 145 aloud with me: "My mouth will speak in praise of the Lord, Let every creature praise his holy name for ever and ever."

DAY TWO: THE PRINCIPLE

The Biblical principle we will study this week is: *'God's power is made perfect in our weakness.'*

There are many times God places us in positions and situations that look absolutely hopeless from our perspective. We look at our circumstances and cannot possibly figure out how God is going to work on our behalf to make this into a good thing. We feel helpless, overwhelmed and completely out of control.

The fact of the matter is more times than not, this is exactly where the Lord wants us. As we look back through Scripture we will see God consistently uses our weakness to show forth His strength. Our weaknesses and the difficulties we face on a daily basis are perfect opportunities for God to show His mighty strength, making it abundantly clear He is the one who does the work, not us.

Of all the men God used as leaders in the history of the Israelites, very few thought they were capable of doing what God called them to do. Moses and Jeremiah both pleaded with God for him to use someone else, feeling completely inadequate to carry out God's commands. They saw themselves as weak, powerless and ineffective leaders who would be relentlessly ridiculed by the very people they were supposed to lead.

Terrified of their call, they pleaded with God to change His mind. When they realized God was not going to get someone else, they finally surrendered themselves in obedience. History has proven the great and mighty things God accomplished through both of these men after they learned to trust in God and not themselves.

Why does God work this way? Why does God always call on the weak and the wanting? So He will get the glory!! How is God glorified when we are able to do everything He asks us by our own strength? If we can do everything we need to do all by ourselves, will we ever need

God? Probably not! Does He want us to not need Him? I don't think so! He wants us to continually rely on Him in all things.

Let's look now at a very familiar story—the story of Gideon. Gideon was another great Israelite leader who saw himself as weak and inadequate. He desperately tried to convince God he was not good enough. God would have to get someone else; he simply was not equipped for the task.

God finally convinced Gideon it was God who was going to do all the work, not Gideon. Gideon was simply an instrument for God to use to lead the battle against the Midianites.

1. Read Judges 6:11–16; 25–27; 7:1–7; 22

    •   What is the first thing the angel of the Lord said to Gideon?

    •   What was Gideon's reply? Did Gideon think the Lord was with the Israelites? Do you ever look at your circumstances and wonder where is God?

    •   How do we know God did not expect more from Gideon than he was able to give?

    •   What were Gideon's reasons for questioning God? Do you ever feel unqualified for the task God has called you?

    •   Where has God promised to be when Gideon goes into battle?

    •   What was Gideon asked to do before he went into battle?

    •   How many men did Gideon start out with as he prepared for battle? How many men did Gideon end up with as he went into battle?

    •   Who claimed the victory for the Israelites?

Oh my, how we can relate to this section of Scripture! I'm reminded of all the times that I, like Gideon, have made up one excuse after another to avoid doing that which was asked of me. Like Gideon, I immediately put up walls of resistance that had to be torn down before God could even begin to work through me.

More than twenty years ago I was a graduate student at Columbia Bible College. After having been there for a few months, the Dean of Women asked me to give my testimony at one of the weekly chapel times.

"No," was my immediate reply.

Not to be discouraged after only one try, she asked again.

"No," was again my immediate reply.

Persistently, she asked again, only to receive the same emphatic response as before.

Finally she asked me, "Ronda, why do you keep saying no whenever I ask you to give your testimony?"

"Because I'm scared to death to get up in front of 500 people and speak."

"You know, God will enable you to do this," she insisted.

"Oh no He won't!" was my reply. "God is not that big."

I never did give my testimony to the school during the chapel times. Consequently, I have spent many, many hours wondering just what exactly I may have missed out on due to my lack of faith and unwillingness to trust God with my weakness.

As I read these verses over and over again, we see that Gideon too, put up similar walls of resistance that prevented God from working through His weakness. Unfortunately, they are the very same walls that we tend to put up in our walk with the Lord. Just as Gideon had to tear them down before he could accomplish God's will, we must too.

Let's see what they are.

1.   The first wall of resistance Gideon put up was his *unbelief of God's presence*. Israel was experiencing a time of severe oppression by the Midianites and Gideon felt abandoned by God. "Where have you been?" asked Gideon.

    We have a tendency to ask God the same question. Our measuring stick of God's love for us is directly related to our circumstances and when they are less then what we would like them to be, we feel as though we have been abandoned. We feel God has forsaken us and no longer hears our cries.

    Max Lucado writes in his book, <u>Just Like Jesus</u>, "Our awareness of his presence may falter, but the reality of his presence never changes." (Pg. 60) Scripture makes it perfectly clear God never leaves or forsakes us. As believers, we are always in a presence of the Almighty. Until we grasp this truth, our doubt of

God's presence in our lives will continue to be an obstacle we will face as we attempt to serve Him.

2.   The second wall of resistance Gideon put up was his own *inferiority*. Gideon did not feel as though he was good enough for God to use him. Christians today face the same obstacle. When asked or called by God to do something, our first response is usually, "I can't do that! I'm not qualified."

When it comes to doing God's work, our abilities or qualifications are a moot point. Serving God is not about what we can do *for* God, but it has everything to do with what God will do *through* us.

All God required of Gideon was to "go in the strength you have." God will supply Gideon with everything else he needs. God will supply us with everything we need, if we will just go in the strength we have. But our inferiority remains an obstacle that most us have a very hard time overcoming.

3.   The third wall of resistance Gideon put up in his service for God was one that we discussed in Chapter One: *idolatry*. I'm hesitant to mention this again for fear of overdriving the point home, but according to Scripture, this is a very important point! Gideon was told to take down his father's altar to Baal and to cut down his Asherah pole. Baal worship and Asherah poles were the predominant religious practices at that time in the region where the Israelites were living. The Israelites were constantly being tempted to worship these other gods along with the One True Yahweh. This eventually led to Israel's demise as a culture and a nation.

Gideon was not only asked to tear down his father's Baal altar and Asherah Pole, he was told to replace them with an altar to the Lord. As we tear down the altars to our idols we can replace them with altars to the Lord by entering into His presence and praising Him. The benefits and blessings we will receive at the foot of our altar of praise will always outweigh those of our idols.

God requires us to worship Him and only Him. We are to take down and destroy anything and everything that prevents us from doing so. Until we do, our own form of idol worship will continue to remain as a wall of resistance in our service to

Him. God cannot work in our lives if we are worshiping any other God. Once Gideon took down his father's Baal altar and Asherah pole, God could use him to carry out His work.

4.   The forth wall of resistance Gideon put up was *placing his security in physical mass*; in his case, it was a large army. He trusted in his army's strength, not in God's. Look how many men Gideon initially gathered to fight against the Midianites: 32,000 men! Does that sound like someone who is trusting in God or in men?

When we face our battles we tend to do the same thing: we put our trust in physical mass instead of spiritual mass. We put our trust in that which can be seen, in that which is most evident. We place our trust in our 401k's. We place our trust in our proximity to family. As long as our spouses are near and not halfway around the world, we will be OK.

We place our trust in our environment: good schools, safe neighborhoods, and our children's extracurricular activities. We are always looking for the perfect place in which to live. I know God wants us to live our lives in an orderly, planned and prepared fashion, but there comes a time when we must do our best and give God the rest. We must trust in our spiritual mass. Our battles may be bigger than we are, but they are not bigger than our God!

2. Read Philippians 4:13; 2 Corinthians 12:9–10

- Through whom can we do all things?
- In which does Paul boast, his strength or his weakness?
- In which do we tend to boast?

When we continue to fight our battles in our own strength and not rely on God, we will always face the issue of our pride. Not until we acknowledge our weaknesses as a 'good thing' will we ever witness the true power of God in our lives.

Gideon went on to face the Midianites in battle with 300 men! Scripture tells us it was God who threw the enemy into confusion and caused them to turn on each other. It was God who caused the victory, not Gideon.

Paul grasped this truth in its totality to the point he delighted in his weakness. He delighted in insults, hardships and persecutions. Paul knew when he was weak, God was strong. He delighted in giving God the opportunity to do great and mighty things. Tomorrow we will look more closely at Paul and how God worked in his life through his hardships and weaknesses.

God will cause many victories in our lives once we tear down our walls of resistance and give him the opportunity to work. God is always present in our lives as He equips us to serve Him fully. We will be utterly amazed at what He will do when we let him.

If that means taking care of our children while our husbands are deployed, God will enable us to do that. If it means moving for the third time in four years, God will enable us to do that. If it means being the caregiver to a very ill loved one, He will enable us to do that.

Day Three and Four: The Proof Of The Principle

Before we begin today's lesson, let's review the principle we studied yesterday: *'God's power is made perfect in our weakness.'*

Gideon felt inadequate and incapable of carrying out the work to which God called him. Due to the hardships the Israelites were facing, Gideon was doubtful God was even present in their lives. Once Gideon removed the idols of his father and trusted in God instead of himself, God was able to work on behalf of the Israelites.

Like Gideon, we tend to view our weaknesses as a negative and try to stay away from situations where we feel inadequate and vulnerable. We never even give God a chance to work in our lives. We tend to put our trust in physical mass; that which can be easily seen, instead of the spiritual mass we all have access to through Jesus Christ. However, once we begin to view our weakness as opportunities for God to display His power, we will truly experience God as we never have before.

Today we are going to jump to the New Testament and take a close look once again at the Apostle Paul. We are going to see how God used what we would call a tremendous weakness to advance the Gospel. What looked as if it would be the end of Paul's ministry actually became a platform from which the Gospel was preached. Letters were written, people came to know Christ, and the Good News spread throughout Europe. Oh, how we must marvel at the way God chooses to accomplish His work.

1. <u>Read Acts 28:16–20; 30; Eph. 6:19,20; Col. 4:3,18; Phil. 1:12–14</u>

   • Was Paul guilty of any crime?

   • Where did Paul live while he was in Rome?

   • Who was chained to Paul 24 hours a day?

Paul had committed no crime nor was he a dangerous criminal, so he was allowed to live in his own house. However, he had an Elite Roman guard chained to him 24 hours a day! The guards most likely took shifts, with each shift lasting six hours. The total number of palace guards who had contact with Paul is probably in the thousands.

Paul was not allowed to go out of his house, but he was allowed to have visitors. These guards observed everything Paul said and did. Conversations and prayers with friends were overheard. Paul's preaching was overheard by those who always kept him in their sight. More than likely the wardens on duty heard songs of praise and worship on more than one occasion. These guards had to be acutely aware of Paul's message: Jesus Christ died for the salvation of all.

If ever there was a time when God worked in an amazing way in the midst of what looked to be a weakness to us, this was it. The Roman guards who watched Paul were the cream of the Roman army. If converted, they could carry the Gospel all over Europe as they were moved from place to place. Paul's chains had become an effective communication tool reminding us that every circumstance in our life can be used by God to fill the earth with the knowledge of the glory of God.

We are much too quick to look at our circumstances to determine whether or not God is working in our lives. What God really wants from us is our total and complete surrender to Him in all things so He can accomplish His work in the way He chooses. He must bring us to a point of complete and utter dependence on Him while we must view our obstacles and weaknesses as opportunities for Him to show us His faithfulness.

   2. Read 1 Corinthians 2:1–5

- How did Paul view himself when he went to the church at Corinth?
- Did he see this as an obstacle or an opportunity?
- Where does Paul encourage his listeners to place their faith?

We must come to see our weaknesses as an opportunity for our faith to be placed in God, not in ourselves or others. God wants to work in our lives, He wants to show himself faithful and He wants to demonstrate to us His miraculous power. I urge you wives of our warriors, don't shy away from your weaknesses. Embrace them. Surrender yourself to God and watch Him work mightily in your life!

DAY FIVE: PRAISE AND PRACTICUM

All week we have studied the principle: *'God's power is made perfect in our weakness.'*

More than anything else, I pray you have changed the way you perceive your hardships and weaknesses. They are not present in our lives just to make us miserable and turn us into champion whiners and complainers. They are present in our lives so we may know and experience the power of God.

As we conclude our study this week, let's read one more verse which illustrates this point. Then we will close the weeks' lesson with a Psalm of praise.

1. Read 2 Corinthians 1:8,9

   - What kind of circumstances does Paul describe in these verses?

   - Would you say Paul faced a few obstacles?

   - What was Paul's 'take' on these hardships?

   - Spend a few minutes reflecting on your life right now. What obstacles are you facing?

   - Are there circumstances in your life that are causing you to question God's presence?

   - Have you completely surrendered this situation to God?

   - Have you acknowledged your weakness and trust in God rather then yourself?

2. Read Psalm 111

   - List some of the glorious and majestic deeds God has done in your life?

   - Do you ponder them, rejoicing in God who made them happen?

   - List the words that describe His precepts and the works of His hands?

   - What is promised to those who follow his precepts?

Praise the Lord for the marvelous deeds He has done in your life. In the times when you feel He has abandoned you, in the times when you feel He has forsaken you, in the times when you feel you cannot overcome one more obstacle, ponder the great and mighty things He has done for you. Delight in them, rejoice in them, treasure them in your heart!

For our practicum today, reflect upon these questions.

1. Try to remember times in your life when you felt weak and ill equipped for the task to which God called you.

    • Did you put up any walls of resistance?

    • Which ones?

    • Did you give God an opportunity to work through your weakness?

    • What blessings did you reap because you trusted God and not your own strength?

    • From this experience, did you learn that serving God is all about what he can do through you and not what you can do for Him?

3. Like Paul in prison, have you ever been in seemingly impossible circumstances, only to be amazed that God actually worked through them?

    • Describe that time.

    • What did you learn from that experience.

    • Did you trust in 'physical' mass or 'spiritual' mass?

    • In which does the Lord delight? One who places his trust in 'the strength of the horse' or 'those who fear him and put their hope in His unfailing love?" (Psalm 147:10,11)

Wives of warriors, I hope you have been encouraged in this lesson to trust God with your weaknesses. He made you just the way you are. Like Gideon, go in the strength you have. He will supply the rest. You will be amazed at what He is able to do through a willing and obedient heart.

Week Five

Forgive Freely

"See to it that no one misses the grace of God and that no bitter root grows up to cause trouble and defile many."

HEBREWS 12:15

In a survey which I took among wives of active duty service personnel, I asked them to describe how they felt about being the wife of a warrior. Most of them marked the words happy, proud, contented, fulfilled, and satisfied.

I found it interesting however, when I asked which emotions they have a hard time dealing with as a result of being the wife of a warrior, those emotions were anger, frustration and resentment. These emotions are usually the result of refusing to forgive something or someone who we feel has wronged us in some way.

In this week's lesson, we are going to address the issue of forgiveness, since the lack of it often leads to anger, resentment and frustration. We will use Scripture to define and illustrate the Biblical principle of forgiveness. We will look at God's forgiveness towards us and realize His forgiveness frees us to forgive others. We will learn what it means to forgive and how important it is to us that we forgive. We will look at the consequences of not forgiving those who have trespassed against us.

We will look a little bit at the emotion of anger; is it good or bad, constructive or destructive? How do we keep it from building up inside us until we explode? How can we turn our anger from negative to positive energy? We'll look at the life of Joseph as an example of addressing these issues.

Let's begin our study on this pivotal topic in our lives!

DAY ONE: PRAISE

For our praise session today we will look closely at the forgiveness we have received from God. Before we can forgive others we must understand the degree to which God has forgiven us. We can forgive freely because we have been freely forgiven of much.

We must first understand the concept of guilt and the difference between being pardoned and being forgiven. When someone is guilty it usually concerns an unalterable past. Although they may be pardoned for their crime, they are still guilty of it. The consequences may be gone but the guilt is not.

The forgiveness we receive from God is more than just a pardon. The forgiveness we receive from God means the sin is gone. We are not only pardoned or excused, but the slate is wiped clean. In the eyes of God it is as if we had never sinned in the first place! We are cleansed as well as pardoned.

Let's take a look at what God has done with our sin.

1. <u>Read Micah 7:18,19; Isaiah 38:17; Isaiah 43:25; Psalm 103:12;</u>
    <u>Psalm 130:3,4</u>

    - Look up the word "hurl" in the dictionary.

    - When God casts our sin into the depths of the sea, how much force does He use?

    - Put something behind your back. Can you see it?

- Look on a map and see how far the East is from the West. Would you say it was a fair distance?

- Think of something you always have a hard time remembering: a birthday, anniversary (hopefully not yours!), meeting times, etc.

- If you cannot remember something, can it be acknowledged?

Oh, what a wonderful truth! The things God has done with our sin! He has hurled them into the depths of the sea. He has put them behind His back. He has blotted them out of his memory, removing them from our record. Imagine how a criminal would rejoice upon hearing there was no record of his transgression, as he stood before the judge, ready to be persecuted for his crime.

I have a terrible memory, particularly when it comes to remembering peoples' names. This does not just happen with people I hardly know, it happens with the women in my Bible studies! I recall many a time I looked directly at someone to ask a question when suddenly, my mind went blank; her name seemingly forever blotted out of my mind, never to be remembered again.

Although always embarrassing, I began to thank the Lord in such times for giving me a demonstration of what He has done with my sin! Just as I could no longer recall a name, He no longer recalls our sin!

Ladies, thank God for what He has done with your sin. We can stand before Him righteous, holy, blameless, free from sin and accusation. The next time we are challenged to forgive someone who has wronged us, let's try to remember the forgiveness we receive from God and know He enables us to freely forgive in the same manner.

DAY TWO: THE PRINCIPLE

The Biblical principle we are going to study this week is: '*We can forgive freely because we have been freely forgiven of much.*'

Before we begin our reading today, let's do a short word study on the word forgiveness. The Hebrew word for forgive is '*Nasa*,' (naw-saw) and means '*to lift, carry off, take away*.' (Strong) In the early life of the Israelites according to the Mosaic Law, the shed blood of a sacrificed animal covered the people's sin but did not take it away. In order for the sin of the people to be taken away, a Priest laid his hands upon a goat, symbolically transferring their sin onto the animal. The goat was then led to a cliff and pushed off. Their sin was completely taken away, never to return. Thus, they were forgiven of their sin.

The Greek word for forgive in the New Testament is '*Aphiemi*' and means '*to let go, to let be, to disregard, keep no longer*.' (Strong) When Jesus became the perfect sacrifice for our sin, our sin was not only covered, it was let go completely!

Let's look back a few weeks to Chapter Two: the lesson on grace. Remember the definition we discussed? Grace means God has bestowed upon us His merciful kindness, not his wrath. It's because of God's grace that He forgives us of our sin.

Let's take a close look at what all this means to you and me.

1. <u>Read Hebrews 12:14,15; Ephesians 4:32; Colossians 3:13</u>

    •   What are we supposed to make every effort to do?

    •   When we do not forgive people, what are they missing?

    •   How can we 'live out' the grace which God has poured out upon us in abundance?

    •   What can happen if we don't forgive someone?

    •   What emotion is described here as a 'bitter root?'

    •   Who has given us an example of forgiveness?

    •   Why can we freely forgive others?

Let me be the first to say, to forgive someone who has wronged us, hurt us, offended us or spitefully used us is about the hardest thing we will ever be called on to do, as a Christian. Forgiving people who have trespassed against us is not something that comes naturally for most of us. Within our fleshly selves and sinful nature, the last thing we want to do is to forgive someone who has hurt us. What we usually want is revenge, punishment, justice, restitution. We want to see the guilty one pay in full for the crime committed against us.

When we are wronged we think people owe us something. They do owe us an apology, but we must understand they cannot pay the entire debt. We tend to hold back forgiveness until we feel the person has paid for their crime, but the truth is, the payment will never be met in full.

Forgiveness means I must carry the load for what happened to me. It's not fair and I don't like it, but that is just the way it is.

I am convinced however, by the power of the Holy Spirit, we can forgive freely. One of my favorite quotes is by Max Lucado from his book, <u>Just Like Jesus</u>. Mr. Lucado writes: "Relationships don't thrive because the guilty are punished, but because the innocent are merciful." (Pg. 22)

Undoubtly the person with the hardest part in the process of forgiveness is the forgiver, not the forgivee. My husband counsels many a couple who are trying to heal their marriage after an adulterous relationship. The person who has been the offender simply says "I'm sorry," while the person who has been betrayed must learn to rebuild a shattered trust.

A friend once called me and asked, "If the person who has offended and hurt me refuses to acknowledge their sin and refuses to say, 'I'm sorry,' am I required to forgive that person?"

"Yes," I replied, "but not for that person's sake. For your own."

As long as we continue to let that bitter root grow up inside us, we remain stuck in the darkness of our own man-made cave. We cannot move forward with our lives. We cannot experience the full blessings of our completeness in Christ while we remain trapped in the snare of unforgiveness.

Tomorrow we are going to look at the life of Joseph and study how he reacted to numerous events in his life that were quite simply, unfair. If anyone had a reason to be bitter, angry and resentful, it was Joseph. But yet through the very worst of circumstances that were none of his doing, he remained faithful to God. He chose to shine instead of whine! And God blessed him greatly for it.

Let's close today with a prayer that God will help us to forgive the person or thing that has made us angry, bitter and resentful. Let's remember the grace that is continually poured out to us and see to it that no one misses its' wonderful work.

Dear Lord,

Thank you for the forgiveness you have given me. You have not only forgiven me of my sin, you have removed my sins far from me. Help me now to forgive those who have trespassed against me with the same grace You have poured out in abundance to me. I cannot do this by myself. I remain angry, bitter and resentful. But with Your help, as I forgive the one who has hurt me, those emotions will heal and perhaps one day, even turn into love. Help me to move forward so that I can accomplish that which You have called me to do. In the precious name of Jesus and for His name's sake, Amen.

DAY THREE AND FOUR: THE PROOF OF THE PRINCIPLE

For the proof of this week's principle, 'We can forgive freely because we have been freely forgiven of much,' we will look at the story of Joseph.

Joseph was a remarkable young man who had a heart for God right from the beginning. The first born to Jacob and his beloved Rachel, Joseph was next to the youngest of all his eleven brothers. Jacob loved Joseph more than any of his other sons and made him a richly orna-mented robe. When Joseph's brothers saw that their father loved him more than any of them, they became very jealous and they hated him.

1. Read Genesis 37

    *   What was Joseph's only 'crime?'

    *   What did his brothers try to do to him?

    *   Where did Joseph end up?

2. Read Genesis 39–41:1

    *   In 39:21–23, who was with Joseph while he lived in the house of Potiphar?

- What did the Egyptian Master do for Joseph?

- In 39:20, when Joseph was put into prison, was he innocent or guilty?

- What did the prison warden do for Joseph while he was in prison?

- In chapter 40:14,15, what is Joseph asking the Chief Cupbearer to do for him?

- Did the Cupbearer follow through on this request?

- How much longer was Joseph in prison?

What a story about unfair circumstances!!! Joseph continues to be punished unfairly by being forgotten by someone who promised to help him out. In the Cupbearer, Joseph may have seen some glimmer of hope that he would soon be free. But that hope quickly vanished when Joseph realized the Cupbearer forgot his promise and failed to mention Joseph to the Pharaoh.

Notice how much longer Joseph remained in prison-two FULL years. Oh, the potential for anger, bitterness and resentment. Having every right to blame someone else for being in that predicament, Joseph continued to shine during his confinement. He continued to prosper, standing out as someone who chose to live beyond his circumstances. How is he able to do this?

3. Philippians 2:14–16

- I call this the 'whine or shine' verse! What are we supposed to do in all circumstances?

- Describe what it means to you to shine in the midst of difficult circumstances?

- When we make the choice to shine in the middle of unfair circumstances, who gets the glory?

No one had a reason to whine more than Joseph, yet as he continued to shine, the Lord continued to bless him. I often wonder if Joseph ever complained or whether he got even the least bit angry. I often wonder if he was ever bitter or resentful. He had to have been just a little, teensy, weensy bit angry about everything that happened to him. Genesis 42:21 tells us that Joseph was 'distressed' and pleaded with his brothers for his life after he was thrown into the pit.

It seems however, Joseph learned to do something we would all be wise to imitate: he directed his anger and energy towards making positive changes. It was as if he knew whining and complaining would not help his situation, it might even make it worse. He refused to let his unfair circumstances take away his faith in God.

Many of you indicated on the survey I took you were angry, frustrated or bitter with the military service. Perhaps you don't like your current assignment and you feel as though you have been in an emotional prison for two full years. We all have the same choice to make that Joseph did as we face unfair situations in our lives. Are we going to whine or shine? Are we going to let our circumstances take away our faith in God?

When I had my horseback riding accident almost thirty years ago, I had the same choice to make. Believe me, I am the Queen of Complaining!! If I thought for a minute that whining and complaining would change my situation and would enable me to get up and walk, I would have whined to the big time.

Somehow I knew making the choice to whine was not the key to living a fulfilled, happy life. I did not know if I was ever going to shine for the glory of God, but I did learn early on to accept what happened to me and get on with my life. God has indeed been with me and has blessed me beyond measure, enabling me to shine for His glory as I hold out the Word of life.

Let's get back to Joseph and see how he finally got out of prison and forgave his brothers for selling him into slavery.

Joseph once again interpreted a dream, this time for the Pharaoh. It was a dream that prophesized seven years of famine followed by seven years of plenty. Upon Joseph's interpretation of this dream, the Pharaoh put Joseph in charge of the land of Egypt. Joseph wisely stored away grain from the years of plenty to be prepared for the years of famine.

It was during the time of the famine when Joseph's brothers came to Egypt to buy food. Here, unbeknownst to them, it was Joseph from whom they bought their food. Joseph recognized them immediately. What follows is an amazing story about forgiveness and reconciliation.

4.   Read Genesis 45:1–15; 50:15–21

- Did Joseph have a 'right' to be angry at his brothers?

- Did Joseph have a right to seek revenge?

- What was Joseph's explanation for everything that happened to him?

- Who had the hardest 'work' to do in this situation, Joseph or his brothers?

- Did Joseph hold a grudge against his brothers?

- Explain Joseph's response in vs. 19 & 20. What does he mean by asking, "Am I in the place of God?"

- Do we have a right to judge others?

Remember Max Lucado's statement? "Relationships don't thrive because the guilty are punished, but because the innocent are merciful." What an example we see here of God's grace and mercy towards those who have wronged us.

Let's end today's session by thanking God He never leaves us or forsakes us. Thank Him He enables us to shine for His glory, even when we have been falsely accused and offended. Thank Him for the joyful reconciliation that comes when we openly and honestly forgive those who have trespassed against us.

DAY FIVE: PRAISE AND PRACTICUM

Where the Old Testament seems to focus on the punishment of Israel's sins, the New Testament focuses on God's forgiveness of those sins. Fifty seven verses in the New Testament have some form of the word forgive in them.

We are clearly commanded to forgive others as we have been forgiven. Forgiving others is our duty and obligation. Some verses even indicate that our forgiveness from God is contingent upon our forgiving others.

1. Read Matthew 6:14,15; 18:35; Luke 6:37; Colossians 3:13

   - These verses clearly tell us our forgiveness from God is in direct proportion to our forgiving others.
   - Who enables us to forgive?
   - Are we able to do this by ourselves?

2. Read 2 Corinthians 2:5–11; 1 John 2:12

   - For whose sake are we to forgive?
   - When we do not forgive, who is 'outwitting' us?

3. Nehemiah 9:17; Psalm 86:5,15; Daniel 9:9

   - What are the words that describe God in these verses?

Praise God He is merciful, compassionate, forgiving, slow to anger and abounding in love!! May our lives reflect the same attributes and characteristics as He transforms us into His image. May we learn that we can freely forgive others because we have been freely forgiven of much!

We have learned forgiveness is the act or state of pardon, remission of our sin, or restoration of a friendly relationship. Next, I want you to think about your own life and reflect upon the following acrostic as you ask yourself the question, "What does it take for me to forgive?"

FAITH	NOT	FEELING
In God, yourself, in others, in the healing powers of the Holy Spirit.		If you wait until you feel like forgiving someone, you will never forgive them. Time only hardens the hurt.

OBEDIENCE	NOT	OBSTINENCE
Ephesians. 4:32-		You may have the right to
Just do it!		be angry, not hostile.

REPENTANCE	NOT	RESISTANCE
The wrong done to you		Sin can never be justified,
may cause you to sin		even if it comes as a
		result of wrong done to
		you.

GRACE	NOT	GUTS
Forgiveness lies beyond you-		You don't have the power,
you must depend on the		strength, nor stamina to
Holy Spirit		do it by yourself.

ILLUMINATION	NOT	IGNORANCE
A vision from God's word,		Popular opinion,
prayer and study will help		legal recourse, etc. is not
		to replace Scripture as the
		basis of your actions.

VIRTUE	NOT	VILLANY
Accepting what happened to you		Getting even before you
and allowing God to work the details.		forgive does not count.

EFFORT	NOT	EASE
Paul says the things I want to do,		Forgiveness will never be
I don't, etc. You can do this with		easy. The flesh will always
the help of the Holy Spirit.		fight against the Spirit.

Think about the following questions:

- Is there someone in your life who has offended you, wronged you or hurt you?

- Have you forgiven them?

- Are you letting that 'bitter root' of anger, frustration and resentment grow up inside you?

- Describe the exhilaration of a joyful reconciliation that occurred when you chose to forgive someone who wronged you.

- Are you in a situation such as Joseph, innocently put in prison for two full years, where you are faced with a choice of whether to whine or shine?

- Do you believe God is with you in this circumstance?

- Do you believe God will work this out for your good, even though right now you feel as though you are being treated unfairly?

Ladies, let's close this week's lesson by thanking God that He is bigger than any difficulties with which we are currently faced. As we forgive others, He promises to forgive us. We *CAN* freely forgive because we have been forgiven of much!!

Week Six

Running The Race

"I press on toward the goal to win the prize for which God has called me heavenward in Christ Jesus."

Philippians 3:14

I'll never forget how shocked I was when I heard the news. The woman who was instrumental in leading me to the Lord completely abandoned her faith! She experienced several miscarriages for which she ultimately blamed God. Never able to understand how a good and loving God would allow her to suffer such extreme emotional pain and heartache, she walked away from God, vowing never to serve Him again.

The cover of a popular Christian magazine recently advertised its featured story, "What to do when your friend turns away from God?" The story sounded much like the one I just mentioned; hard and difficult circumstances followed by years of serving God. "Why bother?" was the response of the woman in the magazine. "If God loved me, this would not be happening."

A. W. Tozer, in his book <u>That Incredible Christian</u>, (pg. 71) writes: "As we move farther on and mount higher up in the Christian life we may expect to encounter greater difficulties on the way and meet with increased hostility from the enemy of our souls. Though this is seldom presented to Christians as a fact of life it is a very solid fact indeed as every experienced Christian knows, and one we shall learn how to handle or stumble over to our own undoing."

In these difficulties we have complete victory in Christ through our enduring faith. This week's lesson is about perseverance through enduring faith: faith that will take us through the worst of circumstances; faith that will see us through to the end; and faith that will enable us to say no matter what, "God is God, God is good."

We will look at how God not only desires us to hang in there, we will learn He also gives us the ability to do that. Just as God calls us to perseverance, He too is a persevering God.

This week we will be reading mostly from the book of Hebrews. At the time Hebrews was written, the newly converted Jewish Christians still believed they needed to comply with the religious laws of their Jewish faith. Although believers in Jesus Christ as the Messiah, they wanted to keep their old Jewish traditions to ensure their salvation.

For those Jewish converts who trusted solely in the supremacy and sufficiency of Jesus Christ, their lives were often marked with persecution and martyrdom, tempting some of them to drop out of the Christian faith altogether. We have lots to learn from the message to these newly converted Jewish Christians about persevering faith.

We will see that our lives as Christians are often compared to that of an athlete: running a race and fighting a fight. The only way to make it to the finish line is to stay in the race! Unfortunately when the going gets tough, too many of us want to quit running the race.

We will learn this week what we must do to stay in the race. Although God gives us the ability, we have some choices to make along the way; there are some actions we must take so we may run more freely without hindrance.

When the race is finished, we will all claim our prize. Both heaven and the believer are being kept for each other. What a glorious day that will be when we are reunited with loved ones who have gone before in the presence of our Heavenly Father.

This is definitely one race I want to finish!!

Let's get started. On your mark, ready, get set, GO!!!

DAY ONE: PRAISE

Let's begin our praise time this week by reading Hebrews 11, commonly known as the 'Hall of Faith.' Since the newly Jewish converts were very familiar with Old Testament Scripture, the author uses many exhortations based on preceding Old Testament passages.

1. <u>Read Hebrews 11</u>

   - What is faith?

   - Why is it essential in the Christian life?

   - Do we have the promise of immediately changing circumstances based on the degree of faith we possess?

   - From these passages, can we draw a correlation between our faith and our circumstances?

   - What has God ultimately promised everyone who believes in Him?

Without faith it is impossible to please God. Faith is believing in something we cannot yet see and being certain of that which we know will come. Faith is expecting the fulfillment of promised blessings and eagerly awaiting their arrival.

Sometimes God rewards people for their faith before they leave this earth and sometimes He waits until He meets them in heaven face to face. Our present day circumstances are not necessarily indicative of the measure of faith we possess.

If you are struggling right now with your faith because of your circumstances or if your feel as though you are on the edge of spiritual ruin, ask God to reveal himself to you. Ask Him to increase your faith so you will be able stay in the race to which he has called you. If you ask him, I believe he will do it!

Ladies, let's thank God for blessing us with faith that will endure for all times!

DAY TWO: THE PRINCIPLE

This week's Biblical principle is: *'God gives believers the ability to keep their faith to the end, regardless of the tests, trials and tribulations.'*

The Greek definition for the word *'persevere'* is *'to continue steadfastly, to endure.'* (Strong) The Bible speaks directly to the perseverance of both God and believers and clearly teaches God gives true believers the ability to keep their faith to the end, through trials, tests, and tribulations.

The Lord's desire and ability to keep us is definitely affirmed in the Scriptures. Eventually believers will come into their promised inheritance. Both heaven and the believer are being kept for each other.

The purpose of this teaching in the New Testament is to focus on the complete faithfulness and reliability of God. Let's look at some Scriptures that illustrate this point.

1. Read 1 Corinthians 1:8,9; Philippians 1:6; 1 Peter 1:4,5; Jude 24; Psalm 17:8

    - Who keeps us strong?
    - Who keeps us from failing?
    - For how long does God promise to do this?

He keeps us strong to the end. He completes the work he began in us. He shields us with his power and keeps us from falling. The believer is strengthened for the conflict against sin in his life as God gives us the ability to make wise choices that keep us from sin. Clearly, God not only wants us to persevere, He enables us to do so.

In Psalms 17:8 we see the psalmist asking God to keep him as the apple of his eye. The Hebrew translation for this phrase is *'the pupil of the eye.'* (Strong) The pupil is a very sensitive part of the eye, essential for vision and must be protected at all costs. The psalmist is asking God to protect and keep him, just as the eye quite naturally protects its pupil. Isn't it wonderful that this is a promise God has already made to all believers?

2.   Read Hebrews 10:19-25

   •   According to this scripture, what five specific actions can we take to help us persevere?
   •   Why are these so important for growth in our Christian walk?

We can draw near to God, hold onto the hope we profess, consider how to spur one another on toward love and good deeds, continue meeting together with other believers and finally, we can encourage one another. Oh, how powerful these actions can be when we are just about ready to give up.

The writer of Hebrews stresses how important it is for believers to help each other by offering support and encouragement during difficult times. As wives of active duty military personnel, we need each other! Those who have made ten moves in twenty years, lived through extended duty deployments during war times and have been left home alone to raise the children can be an immense help for those who are encountering these situations for the first time.

Encouraging one another to remain steadfast in our faith can be an empowering tool that will enable us hold fast to the hope we have when our lives are spinning around. I'm reminded of Jonathan who went to David while David was hiding from Saul in the Desert of Ziph. 1 Samuel 23:16 tells us that Jonathan went to David and helped him find strength in God. Jonathan offers David hope and comfort by encouraging him to look to God. Jonathan then reminds David of God's promises to him.

We too, can encourage our sisters in Christ by reminding them of God's promises to us. The power of an encouraging word to someone in need is not to be underestimated. It can sometime mean the difference in the outcome of a single event.

Today we see God keeps us and gives us the ability to stand firm in our faith. We've looked at some actions we can take that will help us to persevere and hang on. Tomorrow we will look at some other actions which believers are asked to take in order to stand steadfast. We will look at the motives of all believers as well as the method we use to attain our goal. Remember, He who called us is faithful and He will do it!

DAY THREE AND FOUR: THE PROOF OF THE PRINCIPLE

Our reading today is primarily focused on three verses; three power packed verses in Chapter Twelve of Hebrews. The Jewish Christians at that time were being persecuted for putting their faith solely in Jesus Christ. This was a complete break from their orthodox Jewish faith which emphasized the rituals of earthly worship as being the only way to enter into the presence of God. This persecution tempted some of those believers to drop out of the Christian faith altogether.

In the verses we are going to study, Hebrews 12:1–3, we notice the writer persuades these converts to 'hang in there' and not give up on their faith. The victorious life for the believer is achieved by God's grace through perseverance; the continuing steadfastness of the Christian faith.

We would be wise to memorize these verses and hide them in our hearts so we too, will never be tempted to throw in the towel of our Christian life. Right here in these three short verses we are given: (1) A Mandate, (2) A Method, and (3) A Motive.

Those of the faith who went before us cheer us onto victory, looking down from the heavenly realms as though they are watching a race. These are people who kept their focus on God and His promises and are inspiring examples of those who finished the race and claimed their prize, once and for all.

1. <u>THE MANDATE</u>: <u>Read Hebrews 12:1</u>

   - Who are the great cloud of witnesses the writer mentions?

   - What are the two actions Christians are urged to take?

   - What two things are we to throw off?

The Hebrew Christians were given a mandate to take two specific actions: throw off everything and run like crazy!!

In a very literal translation of this verse, I'm reminded of watching the winter Olympics this past year. Every athlete was dressed in a suit that cut down on the wind resistance and allowed them to run the race without hindrance. They threw off everything that might hinder their performance. They were free of additional weight, anything that might bog them down. I'm always amazed when I watch the speed skaters—they even have a hood to cover their heads, intentionally designed to prevent the skater's hair from blowing in the wind and slowing them down!

Spiritually, we are commanded to do the same—throw off everything that slows us down. The King James version reads, *'throw off every weight.'* The Greek translation for the word *'weight'* is *'prominent,'* meaning *'hence a burden, weight, encumbrance.'* (Strong) We become encumbered by our burdens, unable to move. These things are not inherently wrong, but for the faithful Christian, they must be removed.

We tend to be much too wrapped up in the present life. Our care and concern for the present circumstances become as a dead weight upon our soul, preventing us from ascending upwards and pressing forward. We are to throw off anything that takes center stage in our lives, and causes us to be bogged down.

At the time of this writing, God blessed us with a new home. As with all newly constructed houses, initially there are a few 'kinks' to work out. We had a very big 'kink' that totally captured my attention for an entire two weeks.

Until it was all settled I was absolutely miserable, totally unable to concentrate on anything else. I finally asked God to help me throw off this weight and enable me to trust Him with this problem. I was tired of being weighted down to the point it was an effort to physically move!

We are commanded to throw off something else. We are commanded to lay aside the sin that so easily entangles. The King James version refers to, *'lay aside the sin that so easily besets us.'* The term 'to lay aside' in Greek means 'to put off.' (Strong) The action implied here is to give up or renounce. The phrase, *'easily besets us'* means in Greek, *'skillfully surrounding us.'* The second half of this verse then reads: *'Let us give up or renounce the sin that skillfully surrounds us.'*

We know who the author of sin is, don't we? Satan is crafty, deceitful and now we see he is also skillful. He will do anything he can to see us fall to our knees, gasping for breath, unable to make it one more step.

He skillfully surrounds us with that which he knows will tempt us to drop out of the race of our Christian faith.

We have an adversary who would like nothing more than to see us give up and quit. He knows he can never snatch us out of the Father's hand (John 10:28), so the next best strategy to keep us from being a threat to the Kingdom of Darkness is to render us useless for the Kingdom of Light.

He skillfully surrounds us with the sin he knows will cause us to become entangled, unable to move forward. In order for us to run our race in freedom we need to know what our weaknesses are. Satan does. We need to know the areas in which we are most vulnerable so that we can pray for protection and strength to put those things aside and walk away from them. We have a great cloud of witnesses cheering us on to do this.

Satan may be responsible for skillfully surrounding us with that which he knows will tempt us, but he is not responsible for our reactions to it. We must take responsibility for our own actions regarding our behavior.

Colossians 3 is quite clear about the things that so easily entangle Christians in our daily lives. And quite clearly, we are instructed to take actions to avoid them. Praise God that He gives us the ability to do this.

We are instructed to "put to death whatever belongs to our earthly nature: sexual immorality, impurity, lust, evil desires and greed, which is idolatry . . . We must rid ourselves of anger, rage, malice, slander and filthy language from our lips. Do not lie to each other since we have taken off our old self." (Colossians 3:5–9)

Living a life that is free from sin requires discipline on our part. Can we do this totally on our own? Absolutely not! But with the Holy Spirit dwelling inside us we have access to God's power that enables us to renounce them and give them up. Philippians 4:13 tells us that we can do everything through Christ who gives us strength. The power of the Holy Spirit enables us to continue to run our race in freeedom.

When we continue to willfully engage in sinful behavior, we are throwing away God's blessings on our lives. Our sin truly entangles us and keeps us from experiencing God's perfect will for our lives.

Whatever sin with which he so skillfully surrounds us, and it is different for each of us, we are to put it aside and walk away. Sin only keeps us entangled and prevents us from moving forward with full speed. Ladies, whatever is causing you to stumble and lose your balance in the middle of your race, throw it off!! The saints who have gone before us are cheering us onto victory. Free yourself so you can run like the wind, pressing forward to claim your prize.

How are we to do this?

2. <u>THE METHOD</u>: <u>Read Hebrews 12:2; 4:14–16</u>

- On whom are we to focus?
- How is Jesus described?
- What is God's goal for our faith?
- Why did He endure the cross?
- How can Jesus sympathize with our temptations and weaknesses?

The method of every Christian to carry out the mandate of the previous verse is to 'fix our eyes on Jesus' and to follow His example. We have a high priest who understands exactly what we are going through because he has been through the very same things. Just as Jesus focused on the joy that was yet to come, when we keep an eternal perspective of our lives, we are able to throw off everything that hinders us and run the race with perseverance.

We too, can handle our hardships, turn away from our temptations and walk away from our weaknesses because Jesus showed us how. Jesus stayed on course, finished the race and went on to claim the prize! What a wonderful picture of what awaits us!

When I think of what it means as an Air Force wife to run with perseverance the race that has been marked out for us, I think of all the extended deployments on which my husband has been sent.

When he spent a year in Korea, the most difficult months were the last two before he came home. By then we were both worn out and weary of the separation, ready to be reunited as a family. Realizing this event was still a long way off, it was very easy to lose heart, get depressed and remain discouraged.

We decided to focus our attention on our reunion; the wonderful day we would see each other again. Concentrating on homecoming day seemed to help us get through the worst of times. It replaced anxiety with anticipation, it replaced complacency with expectancy and it replaced worry with wonder.

Once my husband returned and our household was back to normal, our reflections upon the year spent apart were that it seemed like a very short time.

It's the same principle with our Heavenly Father. Whenever the going gets tough, think about that glorious day when we shall meet him face to face. At that time your life will seem to have been but an instant. Our lives are far too short to give up in the middle of the race and forfeit our prize.

Just as Jesus sits down at the right hand of the throne of God, we will one day bow down at the foot of the throne, praising God for giving us the ability and the desire to have enduring faith.

3.   THE MOTIVE: Read Hebrews 12:3; 10:36; Philippians 3:12–15

- Why should we persevere instead of drop out of the race?
- Why should we consider what Jesus went through in order to finish the race?
- What are the promises to those who persevere?
- What can we expect when we approach the throne of grace?
- What is our ultimate prize for staying in the race?

The motive to stay in the race is clear: we want to claim our prize! We are encouraged to persevere, not to lose heart or grow weary by considering what Jesus went through. If our Lord and Savior endured so much, (on our behalf!) who are we to think our race should be any less difficult?

We are to press on, no matter what we might be facing. The word in Greek is 'dioko' meaning 'to run swiftly in order to catch a person or thing, to run after.' (Strong) We are to run after the prize for which we have been taken hold, stretching and straining all the way; the glorious prize for which God has called us heavenward in Christ Jesus.

This is the motive that keeps believers in the race of life. It is the promise and hope of what is yet to come: standing in the presence of the Most Holy God and praising him along with the saints of the past!

We've learned this week God gives us the desire and the ability to keep our faith as we run the race until we reach the finish line. His Word gives us a mandate, a method and a motive. By throwing off everything that hinders and the sin that so easily entangles, we CAN run the race with perseverance. As we continue to look to Him and keep Him ever in our focus, we WILL reach our goal. What a glorious day that will be when the believer and heaven are finally brought together in the presence of God.

Makes me want to run an extra lap or two! What about you?

DAY FIVE: PRAISE AND PRACTICUM

As we conclude this week's study, let's review the first three verses in Hebrews Chapter 12 and think specifically of how our lives will change as we apply these verses to our lives.

1. <u>Read Hebrews 12:1–3</u>

    - Is there anything in your life you need to "throw off?"

    - Is there anything that is hindering you from going forward?

    - Is there anything that is holding you back from moving upward spiritually?

    - Are you entangled with a sin with which our adversary has skillfully surrounded you?

    - In the midst of a difficult time, what is your focus?

    - Are you keeping your eyes on the author and perfector of your faith?

    - What kind of joy is being set before you?

    - From our reading on Day Two, what is God's commitment to you?

2.   Read Psalm 73

- What caused this person to fall and stumble while he was racing towards the finish line?

- When you are in the midst of difficult circumstances, are you tempted to focus on the prosperity of unbelievers instead of on Jesus?

- When did the writer begin to understand what was happening?

- How does the writer acknowledge his sin?

- From vs. 23–26, what was the writer's final conclusion about the value of his standing with God?

This Psalm speaks directly to the hearts of most women today. As we run our race stretching and straining, we are tempted to focus on the prosperity of unbelievers instead of focusing on the Lord. A most fatal mistake, we will want to drop out of the race every time. As the Psalmist says, "my feet had almost slipped, I had nearly lost my foothold." (Psalm 73:2)

Not until the writer entered the sanctuary of God did his understanding increase. He was able to regain his footing and stay in the race simply by focusing only on his standing with God.

This is no different for believers today. If we are to regain our footing and stay in the race, we too, must enter the sanctuary of God. We must enter His Word, we must enter into fellowship with other believers, and we must enter into a constant state of prayer.

By the end of the Psalm the writer acknowledges as long as God is with him, earth has nothing of value to offer; certainly nothing worth dropping out of the race. He acknowledges his heart and flesh may fail, as ours often does, but God is the strength and desire of his heart.

Oh, what words to hide in our hearts: Our flesh and our hearts may fail, but God is the strength of our hearts. We will all agree with the Psalmist, who in the midst of difficulties cried out, "It is good to be near God. I have made the Sovereign Lord my refuge." (Psalm 73:28)

1. <u>Read 2 Timothy 4:7,8</u>

    - What was Paul so eagerly awaiting?
    - What is the promise for all who long for God's appearing?

When Paul wrote 2 Timothy, he was nearing his departure from this earth. He fought a good fight, kept the faith and finished the race. The crown of righteousness he so eagerly longed for was about to become a reality. The same crown of righteousness he so eagerly anticipated is the same crown with which we too, will one day be awarded: a crown that we will wear for the rest of eternity.

Ladies, hang in there. Fight a good fight, keep the faith and above all, finish the race. Always remember we were created for eternity, not for today. Today's difficulties and temptations are temporary; eternity is everlasting. Don't throw away the blessings of eternity for today's pleasures.

When we make the Sovereign Lord our refuge, he gives us the ability to stay in the race. We WILL run with perseverance, we WILL remain focused on God, and we WILL make it to the finish line!!

Praise God and Amen!!

Week Seven

Suffering: Hurting and Healing

"As he went along, he saw a man blind from birth. His disciples asked him, Rabbi, Who sinned, this man or his parents, that he was born blind?" "Neither this man or his parents sinned," said Jesus, "But this happened that the work of God might be displayed in his life."

John 9:1–3

*T*his week's lesson on suffering will challenge you more than any other lesson we have had so far. I will tell you right up front, I hold a very unpopular view of suffering.

In this lesson we will study the Biblical facts about suffering so you can begin to think in Biblical terms about this issue. More than likely, each one of us will experience some sort of suffering at least once in our lives. The more we understand how God uses suffering, the better we will be able to accept it when it comes our way.

In my vain attempt to comprehend why so many good, God fearing believers suffer tragic circumstances, I searched the Scriptures through and through, asking the Holy Spirit to help me view suffering from a Biblical Perspective. The results of my research and study are compiled into this lesson.

I must say right off the bat this lesson is NOT meant to explain every difficult circumstance that happens to us and our loved ones. The Bible is clear: the secret things belong to God and we will never understand all of His ways as He works out His plan for our lives. Our finite minds are not capable of understanding the purposes of the Almighty in their entirety.

However, there is enough information in God's word from which we can get a glimpse into His use of suffering in the lives of the people He calls His own. Learning how God used suffering in the past teaches us how He may be using it in the present. By applying the same Biblical principles to our lives today, we can learn to trust Him with the very hardest of circumstances.

Most of us don't like to think of God as one who permits suffering to those who love Him and to whom He calls His children. We like to think of God as kind, compassionate and loving, the giver of all good gifts. I've had people tell me if God is a God who permits suffering, they don't want anything to do with that God.

Although Webster's dictionary describes suffering as '*to undergo pain, hurt, trouble or distress,*' I prefer to think of suffering as our perception that something good is being withheld from us. We view our sufferings as a loss. Either we have lost something or someone, or something or someone is being withheld from us.

In the Garden of Eden, Satan persuaded Eve to take a bite of the forbidden fruit by making the implication God was withholding something good from her. Today, Satan is still trying to convince people that God is withholding something good from them.

In today's Western Culture we don't like to think of suffering as an aspect of the Christian life. Our stuff-oriented society, profuse prosperity and high-tech health care have all contributed to the attitude that suffering is an intrusion into the peaceful life we feel is our right as believers. If we feel as though a life of health, wealth and prosperity has been withheld from us, we often get angry and blame God.

To avoid such thinking, the Biblical perspective of suffering must be taught more widely and frequently in Christian circles.

Wives of warriors, as you study this week I pray the Holy Spirit will speak to you on this very delicate, often controversial subject and lead you into a greater understanding of His word. Remember, the more we know and understand about God will determine what we think and how we act. A clear understanding of the Biblical view of suffering is critical so that we can thrive, not just survive in the midst of them.

Ready? Roll up your shirt sleeves, pull out your shovels and get ready for some digging!

DAY ONE: PRAISE

For today's praise time we are going to focus on the Scriptures that reveal God as kind, loving, good and compassionate. As we strive to know more about this difficult subject of suffering, we must first look at the character of God as He is revealed in His Word.

Deuteronomy 29:29 tells us that, "The secret things belong to the Lord our God, but the things revealed belong to us and our children forever, that we may follow all the words of this law." There is little doubt that God reveals Himself as a God who loves us.

God never promises that our lives will be a walk down Easy Street, but He does promise to always be with us. Psalm 119:50 says, "My comfort in my suffering is this: your promise preserves my life." God never leaves or forsakes us, and for those who call upon His name and trust in His unfailing love, He promises to sustain us.

Let's focus on verses that reveal God as our sustainer during difficult times.

1. Read Psalms 46:1–7

    - How does the psalmist describe God in the first verse?

    - How does this knowledge affect the believer's actions?

    - Hove you ever felt as though your world was giving away?

    - Do you sometimes feel as though your life is as shaky as the mountains during an earthquake?

    - Where is God during this time?

2. <u>Read Psalm 138:7,8</u>

   - What does God do during our times of trouble?

   - What do we usually ask Him to do during times of trouble?

   - What promise does verse 8 give us regarding our difficult circumstances?

3. <u>Read Psalm 22:24–David's prayer of anguish.</u>

   - After a long litany of pouring out his complaints before God, what three conclusions does David reach concerning the character of God?

   - Do you believe God listens to your cries for help, even if your circumstances don't immediately change?

4. <u>Read Matthew 11:28–30</u>

   - What did Jesus mean by saying, 'take my yoke upon you and learn from me?'

   - Was Jesus ever upset, swept away by discouragement or despair in the midst of his suffering?

   - What can we learn from him?

Scripture after Scripture portrays God as a God who is always with us, a God who listens and hears every prayer, and a God who loves those who put their trust in Him. Can you trust Him right now in whatever you are facing?

DAY TWO: THE PRINCIPLE

Yesterday we read about our God who is always with us, always watches over us, always wanting us to run to Him for help. Do not lose that thought as I introduce our principle for this week.

Our biblical principle for this week is: '*Where suffering in the Old Testament was seen as a punishment for sin, suffering in the New Testament is seen as a way to glorify God.*'

My, how we don't like to suffer! Recently I was leading a Bible Study when I asked the question, "What is suffering?" hoping to elicit a response that would include a definition. "When life hurts!" was the very clear and poignant answer.

When life hurts! It seems there is really no other answer to this question. The sad fact is there are many times in our lives when we really, really hurt. We lose loved ones to long, painful illnesses; we lose loved ones to sudden, tragic deaths; we lose jobs; we lose spouses to divorce; we lose our innocent childhoods to abuse; we lose our investments; and ultimately, we lose our focus and our resolve to go on living.

The fact that we suffer is often very difficult to understand, especially for those who believe in a powerful and loving God. Even more perplexing to us is the suffering of those who are helpless or innocent.

We know God can heal ourselves and our loved ones; we know God can fix the situation and we know God can make things better. He is all knowing and all powerful. He speaks the word and everything that is created jumps to obey His command.

But the reality is there are times when He just doesn't speak the word. There are times when He chooses not to heal either us or our loved ones; He chooses not to fix the situation or make it better. The innocent do suffer and at times horrible things happen to good people.

To begin our study, let's look at suffering in the Old Testament.

Perception of Suffering in the Old Testament

Scripture speaks volumes about the suffering of the nation of Israel, God's chosen people. Suffering in the Old Testament was seen primarily as a punishment sent by God as a result of both individual and national sin. This was primarily due to the Mosiac Covenant which promises blessings for obedience and a variety of curses for disobedience.

1.   Read Deuteronomy 11:26–29; 28

     •   Blessings and curses were conditional upon what?

     •   From these Scriptures, how much control did people have regarding consequences/blessings on their lives?

2.   Read Proverbs 3:11,12; Deuteronomy 8:5

     •   Suffering in the Old Testament was also viewed as a form of what sent by God?

Suffering was definitely seen as a cause and effect situation. Each person's suffering was indicative of the measure of guilt in the eyes of God. When people experienced suffering as a consequence of disobedience, it was clearly understood and without mystery.

Only gradually did God introduce the concept that suffering would include the righteous as well as the wicked. As Israel's rebellion and disobediance grew to lengths God could no longer ignore, many righteous people suffered in the punishment that was sent. Clearly, there were times when the wicked prospered and the righteous were afflicted.

3.   Read Psalm 44

     •   From verses 1–8, describe their relationship to God?

     •   Would you call these Godly people?

     •   What happened to the Israelites in spite of this relationship? (vs. 9–16)

     •   How did they feel about this?

     •   Did they have trouble understanding their suffering?

     •   For whose sake do they ask to be delivered from suffering?

This Psalm is a lament of Israel's Godly people after suffering defeat and humiliation at the hand of their enemy. Why God had forsaken them at this time was a complete mystery to them. Suffering was no longer seen only as a consequence to disobedience; suffering included the righteous as well, often without any apparent reason. This left people feeling confused, weak and vulnerable.

In the book of Job we get a closer look at someone who was righteous, yet suffered tremendously. As Job, his wife and his friends all tried to make sense out of the suffering that Job was experiencing, it was hard for them to understand that God actually allowed or permitted the righteous to suffer.

Surely there was some hidden sin in Job's life of which he was unaware. The fact that Job would suffer while being righteous was a dichotomy of their orthodox thinking.

The Old Testament view of suffering as a punishment for man's sins did not change until after the death and resurrection of Jesus Christ.

Perception of Suffering in the New Testament

God came to earth in the form of Jesus Christ and suddenly, suffering takes on a whole new meaning. Once thought of as the consequence of sin and disobedience, Jesus was tempted and suffered more than we ever will, yet, He was without sin!

4. Read 2 Corinthians 5:21; 1 Peter 2:22; 1 John 3:5

    • What do these verses tell us about Jesus and sin?

Clearly, Jesus was sinless. Sin was not in Him. He had no sin. Yet, he suffered immensely at our expense. The Old Testament theory of cause and effect suffering is suddenly blown out of the water!

Let's take a moment to look at the suffering endured by our precious Savior during his short life here on earth. There are a lot of verses to look up—Jesus endured a lot of suffering!

5. Read the following verses and list the sufferings of Jesus:

    • John 1:11; John 7:1,5
    • Luke 4:1

- Matthew 2:16; John 5:16; John 8:58
- John 13:21
- Matthew 26:69–75
- Matthew 15:16; 16:6–11; John 10:6
- John 18:12; Matthew 26:57; Mark 15:1
- Luke 23:1,2
- Luke 23:36
- Matthew 26:67
- Matthew 27; Mark 15; Luke 23; John 19
- Hebrews 2:10

He was born into poverty, rejected by those he was sent to save, denied and deserted by his friends and followers, threatened constantly by the leaders of the day, falsely accused numerous times, endured physical torture and humiliation, suffered excruciating pain on the cross and suffered the ultimate trial that you and I as born again believers will never experience—he was forsaken by God, the Father. Jesus' sufferings made him able to empathize with our sufferings.

Jesus prepared his disciples numerous times for his coming suffering and death, however, it was not until after his resurrection that his followers finally understood that as co-heirs with Him, they were to share in his sufferings as a pre-requisite to sharing in His glory.

6. Read I Peter 4:12,13; Romans 8:18; Philippians 3:10,11; 2 Corinthians 4:17

    - What is the common theme in these verses? *'The eternal glory that outweighs them all!'*

In spite of everything Jesus taught on the necessity of suffering, the Old Testament orthodox view of suffering as a punishment for sin still prevailed during the time of his earthly ministry.

7. Read John 9:1,2

    - What was the perceived reason for this boy's suffering?

Once understood, the necessity of Jesus' sufferings and the sharing of them by his disciples became a widely discussed topic in the Epistles. Where the Old Testament promised health, wealth and prosperity for obedience, Christ, as well as his apostles, expected afflictions to be a part of their daily Christian life.

8. <u>Acts 14:22; Philippians 1:29</u>

- What came to be expected for following Christ?

Suffering is to be Expected

Clearly, suffering is to be expected as we walk with Christ. There will be times in our lives when we will hurt. Suffering is inevitable; it is going to happen. It is not a question of IF we will suffer, it is a matter of WHEN.

As we go throughout our lives, trials and tribulations will come; we will all have our mountains to climb at one time or another. Our mountains will be different and some of them are even invisible; but there is no such thing as a trouble free life for saint or sinner.

Please, do not close your books at this point and leave the room in total despair. The saints have the indwelling power of the Holy Spirit to help them overcome and endure all suffering!

The more we understand about suffering, the more we will choose to depend on God to help us accept it as part of His plan for our lives. Although we will never know all the answers to why we suffer, through Scripture, the Holy Spirit leads us to understand how we can view our suffering as a means of God's grace.

For days three and four, we will study the proof of this difficult principle by recognizing a few of the sources from which our suffering comes, as well as some of the reasons that God allows them.

Hang in there, wives of warriors!! I know this is a difficult subject. But we must never forget we serve a loving, gracious and powerful God who enables us to face the most difficult challenges with boldness, confidence and trust in his unfailing love.

Day Three and Four: The Proof Of The Principle

Yesterday we looked at various aspects of suffering. We looked at a definition of suffering: the perception that something is being withheld from us. We looked at how God used suffering in the Old Testament: primarily as a punishment for sin and disobedience. We studied the sufferings of Jesus: one who suffered greatly, yet was without sin. And we looked at how God used suffering in the New Testament: primarily as an experience to share in the eternal glory of God.

Today we are going to look into some of the sources of our sufferings as well as some possible reasons for them. As I said earlier, we will never be able to explain ALL suffering, however, as we look closer at how God uses suffering, we may find some clues that will help us understand it better.

Let's look at the sources of suffering first. Where does suffering come from?

Sources of Suffering

1. <u>Read Genesis 3:16–19; Read Romans 5:12; Matthew 15:19; Romans 3:23.</u>

   - What is the source of suffering in these verses?
   - Explain how the consequence of Adam's sin effects us all.

Clearly, sin and disobedience were the first source of both physical and emotional suffering. God never intended for this to be a part of our human experience, but suffering was brought to the human race through the sin and disobedience of Adam and Eve. No matter what race, religion, ethnic background, social or economic status, every human being will experience some degree of sorrow and suffering due to our sinful nature.

The imputation of Adam's sin (Adam's sin being 'charged' to the rest of us) and the consequences of it extends to the entire human race. Along with this guilt comes a corrupt nature, from which all sin originates. No one is free from involvement in sin.

2. <u>Read Job 2:7; Luke 22:31,32; 2 Corinthians 12:7–9</u>

   • What is the source of suffering in these verses?

Satan is a source of suffering. We are in spiritual warfare and one who belongs to God can expect an attack. Satan's sole purpose is to thwart the plans and purposes of God and he does that by assaulting the very vessels through which God works—His people! He constantly tests us, hoping to bring us to spiritual ruin.

If Satan's ploys against us can cause us to lose our focus, weaken our resolve or cause us to feel alienated from God, he has made a significant impact that hinders God's work from being accomplished.

In a later chapter we will study spiritual warfare in greater detail. Suffice it say right now, the times in my life when I have experienced the greatest 'hits' from our adversary were those times just before God was getting ready to do something through me that would further His kingdom.

In one of our moves to a new assignment where we were sure that God had a great work for us to do, the physical move itself was a nightmare! Broken furniture, broken computers, and endless delays in getting services and utilities hooked up so that we could get on with the work that God would have us to do could have easily caused us to just give up.

The frustration of our move was almost overwhelming. There seemed to be no end to it. The fog of physical exhaustion can get so dense that you tend to forget that which you know to be true about God and his word. Satan is definitely out to defeat us and knows the exact pressure points where we are weak and vulnerable.

I love Jesus' response to Simon in Luke 22:32: "But I have prayed for you Simon, that your faith may not fail." This speaks mightily about how God permits Satan to cause us suffering. But as He does, *He prays for us!* He does not leave us stranded, unattended and forsaken. <u>The Holy Spirit offers refreshment in the midst of all suffering</u> if we will only lift our focus from our situation and look to Him.

3.   <u>Read Psalm 41:7; Psalm 55:2,3</u>

• Who has caused the Psalmist's suffering?

his enemies

Suffering comes from other people. Unfortunately, we often are hurt both physically and emotionally by the people in our lives, usually by those who are the most dear to us.

Some people deliberately hurt us while others do it unintentionally. Scripture tells us that we are naturally envious, jealous and malicious towards one another. It is only with the intervention of the Holy Spirit living in us that we can treat each other with love and respect.

Even for those whose lives are committed to the Lord, they are still subject to human emotions and to the behaviors that result from them. We are not perfect people and never will be until the return of the Lord Jesus Christ.

People who are envious and jealous of us react to us in strange ways, while some people are simply mean-spirited. As innocent as we may be, we are often the victims of other people's rage, incompetence, and inadequacies.

On the other side of the coin we must realize that we, too, are probably the cause of other people's suffering. Whether we like it or not, our words and actions have a direct effect on those closely related to us.

When we knowingly engage in unhealthy activities we may be ready to accept the consequences for our own lives, but the consequences that are sometimes paid by our innocent family members because of a mistake that we made can be even more devastating to everyone involved.

In Colossians 3:12–17, Paul gives us clear instructions on how to live with each other and how to treat other people. Talk about a way to eliminate one source of unnecessary suffering!

4.   <u>Read Proverbs 1:31; 10:4; 10:21</u>

• Who is the cause of suffering here?

The wicked; fool; those who don't seek knowledge.

Suffering comes as we bear the consequences of our own errors or foolishness. We overeat, overspend, over indulge ourselves in a number of worldly pleasures and then are surprised at the mess in which we find ourselves.

My husband spends a large part of his day counseling people of all ages and backgrounds. Most of their time is spent trying to un-do the harm caused to themselves and others by bad decisions that were made concerning major life activities.

Often when this happens we tend to blame our suffering on someone else. We must understand that we are fully capable of sinning all by ourselves without the assistance of either Satan or others.

We've looked at some of the sources of suffering. Now let's look at some of the reasons for suffering.

Reasons for Suffering

There is meaning and purpose to our suffering. When the circumstances appear meaningless and tragic, God is at work. He wants to be at work in our lives to turn our greatest tragedies into triumphs. Understanding this truth makes our suffering somewhat easier to endure, particularly during the times when we don't have a full understanding of the ultimate question we all have in times of trouble—"why?"

1. Read John 9:3; John 11:45

    *   What is the purpose of this man's blindness? *So the work of God might be done in him.*
    *   What the purpose in Jesus' 'delay' in coming to Lazarus? *To perform a miracle so their faith will increase.*

All suffering on the part of Christians is for the glory of God. God is glorified when His work is displayed in our lives. Usually the more we suffer, the bigger our audience. That means more people may learn of His power and come to know Him as their own Lord and Savior.

In the case of Jesus raising Lazarus from the dead, He purposely delayed His coming so that by the time He got there, many Jews would have already gathered. God received greater glory and many Jews put their faith in Him.

2. Romans 8:18; I Peter 4:12

    *   To what does Paul compare his suffering? *With spending eternity with God in heaven.*

Our suffering helps us to have an eternal perspective on life. We know that our lives here are but an instant. Suffering teaches us just how fleeting this life really is.

Paul was not ignorant or blind to the sufferings of human existence. He experienced more suffering than any of us will ever know. Yet, he was willing to endure them because of the future hope and glory that he knew was his. To the degree that we suffer here on earth, we will rejoice that much more when we get to heaven. Don't you know that I will rejoice with great joy once I receive my heavenly body that will not need a wheelchair for mobility!

Our faith is strengthened during our times of suffering as we consider the glory of God that will one day be revealed. No matter what difficulties we may be facing, one day we will all meet Him face to face. We will be overjoyed when we realize that our sufferings have ended and that we have been found 'faithful at the post.' I am looking forward to that day!

3. Read Hebrew 12:5; Proverbs 3:11,12

- What is the purpose of suffering here? *for discipline, as a father corrects his son he loves.*

God disciplines us through our suffering with the purpose of making us more like Him. God is continually refining the character of His children to equip them for His service. So many times we are just not ready for what the Lord has planned for us and it takes some Godly discipline to get us back on track. A wise servant who desires that the Lord use him to accomplish His purposes will be open and responsive to the Lord's discipline, knowing that it is for the best.

4. Read James 1:2–4; Romans 5:3–5

- What is God's goal through suffering? *– to develope perseverance, character, and hope.*

Every circumstance in our life is designed to make us more like Him. God's ultimate goal for us is to conform us into the likeness of His son. As much as we don't like it, He uses our suffering to achieve that goal.

Suffering produces Godly character when we are receptive to it. Many times when my son is unhappy about a situation, and he is agonizing about it with me, my response is, "Toby, God is building your character." A Christian can rejoice in his sufferings because he knows that it is not meaningless.

5. Read 2 Corinthians 1:3–7

    •   What purposes does suffering fill in these verses?

for the comfort God gives us in our sufferings overflows out of us onto others who also need comfort.

Suffering equips us to help others in their suffering. Our own experience can make us more compassionate towards others.

I have a friend who recently became a certified Physical Therapy Assistant. Before he even began his first job, he tore his rotator cuff in a sports injury and needed surgery so that it could be repaired. After four weeks of keeping his arm in a sling, he will need intensive physical therapy. Don't you know that he will be much more compassionate and sympathetic towards his patients than he would have, had this not happened to him.

I have several friends who are breast cancer survivors who all spend their free time ministering to those who are in the middle of chemotherapy and radiation treatments.

When I needed major surgery last year, the first thing I did was to find someone who had been through the same procedure.

Yes, we do indeed suffer so that we may be a comfort to other people.

6. Read 1 Peter 3:15

    •   For what purpose do we sometimes suffer?

to witness with others the work that God is doing in our lives.

Suffering is a form of witness. Christians are not only sustained by God's grace during their suffering, they often grow spiritually in their walk with the Lord. Fellow Christians are lifted up and the unsaved are convicted as they watch God working in other's lives.

My wheelchair has become an instrument through which I can readily testify to God's sustaining love and grace. I call it my 'standing stone,' taken from Joshua chapter four. Suffering can be the 'standing stones' in each of our lives, reflecting attention to God for people who would otherwise not see Him.

7. Read 1 Peter 1:6,7; Malachi 3:2–4; Isaiah 1:25

    •   Is God's purpose here to make us bitter or better?

to make us better.

We are all tested in our faith at some time or another in our lives. It's God's intention that our testing be used for our good, to refine and strengthen our faith. Just as a muscle must be exercised to achieve maximum strength, so our faith must also be exercised. Just as physical exercise involves pain, so does spiritual exercise. I'm reminded of the phrase, "no pain, no gain." That applies to our spiritual life as well.

Remember the sanctifying grace that we studied back in Chapter two? It's the same principle at work here. Again, we must remember *"God wants to use us, not abuse us."*

The Most Difficult Suffering

The most difficult suffering of all is that for which we can find no reason or explanation. We can endure almost anything if we feel there is a higher purpose for which we are suffering. The anguish of meaningless suffering affects every aspect of our lives.

Our trust in God during difficult times should never rest in our ability or inability to figure out His mind and purpose. We will never know or understand the reasons why those who trust God suffer until we meet the Lord face to face. We are just not capable of understanding everything that He is doing in our lives.

There will be hardship and suffering that we will never fully understand. God works in our lives as He desires, regardless of whether we understand that working or not. Our trust must be placed in the revealed nature and character of God.

Wives of warriors, this concludes our lesson for day three and four on proving the principle that the New Testament teaches us suffering is used to bring God glory. Whew!! As my husband sometimes says, "I'm plumb give out."

I know you have had to look up a lot of Scriptures, but I pray God has spoken to you through them. Tomorrow we will spend our Praise time thanking Him that He is Sovereign, in control of ALL things, and is a good, loving and gracious God.

DAY FIVE: PRAISE AND PRACTICUM

We've spent most of the week delving into the Scriptures seeking to understand more clearly God's use of suffering in the lives of believers. We've learned much about the Biblical view of suffering. It's my prayer now that we can put these principles into practice as we encounter suffering in our own lives.

For our Praise time today as we close this week's difficult lesson, let's read Psalm 139. It is a combination of revealing the greatness of God's character in light of the reality of the human experience. We can trust God in all things because He knows us, He created us, He is with us, and He guides us.

1. Read Psalm 139 interactively

    -   Describe how God knows us. *He knows every detail; He knows us intimately.*
    -   Since when has He known us? *Before we were born.*
    -   Is there any running from God's presence? *No*

    -   What is the Psalmists one desire? *To know the thoughts of God; to be close to Him.*

For our Practicum today, reflect upon the difficult circumstances in which you have found yourselves from time to time. Think upon the principles we have studied this week and ask the Holy Spirit to help you apply them to your situation.

    -   In your suffering, can you relate to one of the possible reasons we discussed? *Other people have been the cause of my suffering; wrong choices.*
    -   Can you pinpoint the source of your suffering? *Yes.*
    -   After studying the sufferings of our Savior, are you more willing to accept what is happening to you, particularly if there is no apparent reason for it? *Yes.*

- Are you willing to let God have His way with you, trusting Him that this is for His glory? Yes.

- In the difficult times when God just does not make sense, will you trust in His revealed, loving nature? Yes.

Wives of the warriors, this concludes our study on suffering. God Bless you all for rolling up those shirt sleeves, pulling out those shovels and digging deep into God's word.

May God bless you all richly as you continue to serve Him by serving our country in the most honorable position of the wife of a warrior!

Week Eight

Spiritual Warfare

"For our struggle is not against flesh and blood, but against the powers of this dark world and against the spiritual forces of evil in the heavenly realms."

Ephesians 6:12

*T*his week's topic, spiritual warfare, is a topic that simply cannot be overlooked in this study. In my research associated with writing this Bible study, every book I read addressed the issue of spiritual warfare and the conflict in which we are bound to be engaged at some point in our spiritual walk.

The fact that we live in a spiritual realm as well as a physical realm is very clear. While the physical realm we live in is very tangible, the spiritual realm is not. Just because we cannot see, touch or smell it does not mean it does not exist. We would be wise to be aware of its existence, along with the battle that is continually taking place within its borders.

As we will find out in our study, we have an adversary who would like nothing better than to render us useless for the Kingdom of God. We will look closely at some of his tactics later in the week, but we find out right away he chooses times when we are most vulnerable to lure us out of our protective circle. For myself and many others, this happens most during the times of greatest stress.

According to the 'Richter scale of stress,' wives of warriors are constantly facing extremely stressful situations: moving, finding housing, getting kids relocated in school and other activities, finding employment, single parenting, dangerous duty assignments for our spouses. We need to know what it means to 'put on the full armor of God so that you can take your stand against the devils schemes' (Ephesians 6:11), especially during these particularly stressful times.

For those of us who are called into Christian work and ministry, we will certainly face times of spiritual opposition. We will experience spiritual oppression. It is not a matter of *if*, but of *when*. Knowing what can happen and being able to recognize it when it does happen enables us to stand our ground from our victorious position in Christ.

Let me say right from the start I have no intentions of glorifying Satan and the havoc he has wreaked in many a life. My purpose for including this topic in this study is to prevent him from doing more damage than he has already done. As one who seems to thrive the most when he is ignored, denied or underestimated, increasing our awareness of his existence and the limited power he really has over us will help us to be victorious in our Christian walk.

As wives of warriors we quickly learn from our husbands there are two very important rules in warfare. Rule #1: *Know your enemy!* Our military forces today spend enormous amounts of time and money getting to know the very one from whom we feel the greatest threat. We learn their language, we learn their culture, we learn their geographical location, we learn who their friends are, we learn about their military capability. We learn everything we possibly can in order to defeat them, should we ever meet them in battle.

Many Old Testament warriors used this same war logic. Moses sent out 12 spies to learn what he could about the people who were living in the Promised Land. Joshua sent two spies to learn more about his enemy before he overtook Jericho. Gideon himself went to spy on the very people he was about to attack. We see from the very beginning how important it is to know our enemy!

Warfare Rule #2: *Use your weapons!!* My husband has spent more hours than he has cared for learning how to use a gas mask. He has spent time in an enclosed chamber filled with poisonous gas, not only to learn how to use a gas mask, but to trust in its capability to protect him. In this lesson we will look closely at the weapons we have at our disposal and more importantly, we will learn to trust in them as we encounter our Spiritual enemy.

The first step we must take in our quest to 'know our enemy' is to acknowledge the fact that Satan really exists. Contrary to God, who wants to make himself known to people, Satan would prefer people deny his very existence. As we look around the world today it seems he has been somewhat successful with that game-plan.

He is portrayed most often as a red-faced horned creature, holding fast to a pitchfork. From the liberal pulpits we hear that a belief in Satan is pure baloney. From the conservative pulpits we hear very little.

I agree with Dietrich Bonhoeffer who wrote in his book, <u>Spiritual Care</u>, before his death in 1945, "Pastoral care has been dominated by psychological methods and language." (Pg. 23) Spiritual care, which concerns itself with how the Word of God deals with us, has been confused with pastoral care.

It's time to face reality: we have an adversary who walks around like a lion, looking for those whom he may devour. We would be wise to learn more about him!

During this lesson we will look closely at the existence of Satan in the heavenly places. Even Jesus acknowledged his existence on numerous occasions. We will look at the meaning of the word *'power'* and differentiate between God's power and Satan's power.

We will study Satan's weapons and most importantly, the protection the believer has against them. We will learn about the weapons we have at our disposal and how we can trust in them. We will learn we have already won the battle! It is from a victorious position in Christ that we fight the good fight of faith. We are not fighting to gain the victory, we are fighting to keep it!

Let's begin our study!

DAY ONE: PRAISE

As always, we will begin the week with a day of reading praise verses interactively. We will read Psalm 91, a Psalm that describes the keeping power of the Father concerning his children on earth. This is a Psalm that vividly expresses the security of those who trust in God. During Jesus temptation in the wilderness, Satan quoted verse eleven of this Psalm. As you read it, thank God for His love and protection for every believer.

1. Read Psalm 91 interactively

    - List the words used to describe God in the first two verses? "Most High", "Almighty", 'refuge', 'fortress'.
    - What does this mean to you? I can go to him in trouble.
    - What is a shield? What will be the believer's shield from the enemy? Keeps the enemies arrows (weapons) from hurting you. God's faithfulness
    - What will be lacking in the believer when he trusts in God? Fear, disaster.

    - Read Psalm 34:7

    - How does the Lord protect believers? With the angel of the Lord.
    - List the promises of God to those who truly love and trust him. They will be protected.

    - From reading this Psalm today, should believers fear what Satan could do to them? No.

As we study more about spiritual warfare this week, you will want to know as believers we are promised protection from the enemy. God keeps us under his wings, he keeps us in his care and he keeps us behind his shield of faithfulness. The fiery arrows of the enemy will come at us from all sides, but none will hit their target. They will fall to the ground and burn out, having missed their mark completely.

Praise God we have such a protector!

DAY TWO: THE PRINCIPLE

The principle we will study this week is: *'Greater is He who is in you than he who is in the world.'* (1 John 4:4)

Satan's existence may not be acknowledged by the world we live in today, but it is certainly acknowledged in the Word of God. Satan is acknowledged in seven Old Testament books, nineteen New Testament books and is referred to by every New Testament writer. He is mentioned approximately fifteen times by Jesus Christ himself.

1. <u>Read the following verses:</u>

   - Matthew 4:10
   - Matthew 16:23
   - Matthew 25: 41
   - Luke 10:18
   - John 8:44
   - John 6:70
   - Luke 22:31

Clearly, Satan does exist. To deny the existence of Satan is to deny the very words of the Lord Jesus himself. But where does he live?

The book of Ephesians speaks of the 'heavenly places' or 'heavenly realms.' This phrase is used five times throughout the book. Basically, the heavenly places are the invisible reality in which the believer now lives, in contact with God and in conflict with Satan. Most of the Christian issues we face will be resolved in this invisible realm.

2. Read the following verses:

    - Ephesians 1:3
    - Ephesians 1:20–22
    - Ephesians 2:6
    - Ephesians 3:10
    - Ephesians 6:12

From these scriptures, we see the heavenly places are the seat of Christ's power and glory. They are also the headquarters of the principalities and powers of evil. Just how much power does Satan have in these heavenly realms?

We must do a word study on the word *'power.'* There are many words used in the Greek language for the English word *'power.'* We will take a close look at two of them.

One is *'Dunamis'* and the other is *'Exousia.'* They are both used extensively throughout the New Testament, however each has a very different meaning. Understanding the difference of their meaning is essential in order to understand the difference in Christ's power and Satan's power.

The word *'Dunamis'* means *'power residing in a thing by virtue of its' nature, power for performing miracles, strength, ability.'* (Strong Concordance) This is the power that is associated with God and Jesus Christ.

3. Read the following verses in Ephesians where the word 'Dunamis' is used.

    - 1:19
    - 1:21
    - 3:7
    - 3:16
    - 3:20

This *'Dunamis'* power is based on the actual strength and ability of God. There is no greater form of power than *'Dunamis'* power. The power mentioned in Ephesians 1:20, the incomparably great power that God exerted when he raised Christ from the dead, is *'Dunamis'* power. This is the same power that works in us through the Holy Spirit.

The word 'Exousia' means 'the power of authority or right, the power of rule or government, the power of him whose will and commands must be submitted to by others and obeyed.' (Strong Concordance) This power is in the form of legal power as opposed to force, ability or strength. This is different from the power of God mentioned in the verses we just read in Ephesians.

'Exousia' power needs someone to give that power to them. For example, I live next door to a State Trooper. If I was doing something illegal, Mr. State Trooper has the power to come over and arrest me. He has been given this power by the state of Virginia. The neighbor on the other side of me does not have this power and so therefore, has no control over me.

The power that Satan has is the 'Exousia' power! He only has power over us if we allow him to have it. If we do not give him the power to influence our lives, he is powerless to do so. Satan is a bully taking advantage of those who allow themselves to be bullied.

4. <u>Read the following verses in Ephesians where the word 'Exousia' is used:</u>

   • 1:21

   • 2:2

   • 3:10

   • 6:12

In each of these verses we see Satan only has the kind of power that needs to be given to him. If we, as believers, never allow him to have authority and rule over us, he will never have it!

I find this very exciting. This study leads me from being afraid of Satan and what he can do to me to being comforted by the fact that the power in me is far greater than the power he will ever have *over* me. Is this great or what!

I hope you have been encouraged by today's study. Tomorrow we will learn about Satan's tactics as he tries to bully us into a state of uselessness for the Kingdom of God. Above all else, never forget that He who is in you is greater than he who is in the world.

DAY THREE AND FOUR: THE PROOF OF THE PRINCIPLE

Yesterday, we studied Rule # 1 of spiritual warfare: *Know your enemy!* For the next two days we will study Rule # 2: *Use your weapons!*

Part of knowing your enemy is finding out what weapons they have at their disposal, so we are going to start today's lesson doing just that. We are going to take a look at the arsenal Satan has stored up in his bunker and uses against us without a second's hesitancy. So how does the bully of the playground push us around?

He has two types of weapons: Psychological and Physical. His psychological weapons are far more damaging to us than his physical weapons. Harder to pinpoint and harder yet to overcome, we will take a look at these first.

Satan's Psychological Weapons

1. <u>Read the following verses and note the psychological weapons Satan uses against people:</u>

   - Amos 6:1

   - 2 Corinthians 11:3,4

   - Proverbs 6:14,19

   - James 1:13–15

   - Galatians 5:7–10

   - Ephesians 3:13

   - Joshua 8:1

   - Isaiah 45:10

This is only a partial list of the psychological damage Satan has inflicted upon his unsuspecting targets. Please feel free to add any other psychological weapons he has used against you in the past that I may have overlooked. At one time or another we have all fallen victim to his shrewd schemes.

Fear, discouragement, despair, complacency, deceit, dissention, confusion and temptation are all part of his plan to cause us to become spiritually unhealthy. Just as the soldier who is physically unfit cannot even engage in the battle, so it is with us spiritually. Satan's goal is to destroy our power to engage in spiritual warfare. If we are spiritually crippled and cannot even participate in the battle, he has already won the war!

Now, let's take a look at his physical weapons.

Satan's Physical Weapons

Without the intervention of the Holy Spirit we are helpless in our defense against the cravings of our flesh. The characteristics of that nature are explicitly spelled out in Scripture. Satan has a field day with these self-destructive behaviors in those who choose to participate in them.

2. <u>Read the following verses and note the physical weapons Satan uses against people.</u>

   • Galatians 5:19–21
   • Colossians 3:5

This is also a short list of these weapons which he fires directly at people when they are most vulnerable. Add to the list alcohol, drugs, and pornography and you have a whole gamut of tricks Satan will use in a heartbeat if he thinks someone will eventually give in and try them.

We've looked at the weapons of Satan. We all know he is not afraid to use them on any of us at any time. But remember: *WHO HAS THE GREATER POWER? WE DO!* He can only inflict this damage on us to the degree that we let him.

Now, let's move on to the most exciting part of this lesson: the weapons of the believer!! These are far, far greater and more powerful than those of our enemy. We are going to focus on three weapons in particular and more importantly, we will learn how to use them!

The Believer's Weapons

3. <u>Read the following verses and note the weapons of the believer:</u>

- Ephesians 6:16; 1 Peter 1:5
- Colossians 4:2; Ephesians 6:18,19
- Ephesians 6:17; Matthew 4:1–11; Psalm 119:11

These weapons may be invisible, but powerful they are. Faith, prayer and the word of God. Let's start with the first weapon of faith. What does it mean to put on the shield of faith?

We have already compared God's power with Satan's power. God has already overcome our foe because His power is greater than our enemy's. In Him, we are more than conquerors. (Romans 8:37) We have already been given the victory. (1 Corinthians 15:57) Ephesians 1:22 says 'He has put all things under his feet.'

We must first begin to see ourselves in Christ and already standing in the victorious position. We must accept this victorious position BY FAITH. Not until we have done that can we even be prepared to engage in spiritual warfare.

From this point on we fight, not to attain the victorious position, for it is obtained the moment we stand in Christ, but to keep it. We have already attained a superior position to our enemy. Our struggle now is to hold our ground.

I have drawn a diagram below that illustrates the shield of faith.

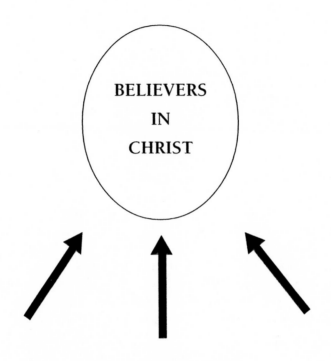

SATAN'S FIERY DARTS

As you can see from the diagram above, we *'who through faith are shielded by God's power'* are guarded and protected from Satan's fiery darts. Within the impenetrable shield of faith we are protected from our foe on all sides. As long as we remain in Christ, Satan is powerless over us. From the youngest Christian convert to the most mature believer, we are shielded from Satan's arrows. It is only when we jump outside the circle or allow Satan to lure us out, that we become vulnerable to the attacks of the devil.

4. Read the following verses from Psalms about God being our shield:

- 3:3
- 5:11,12
- 7:10
- 18:2,30
- 28:7

By faith, God is our shield. As long as we remain in Him, we will always be protected from our enemy.

The second weapon we will look at that the believer has at his disposal is *PRAYER*. Notice how many times Paul exhorts us to pray in the verses in Ephesians alone.

Prayer is a very dangerous weapon to be hurled at our enemy. The praying Christian has direct access to the throne of God and to the power that accompanies that position. Satan finds this very unsettling. He never knows from which direction the danger will come. He knows that ALL THINGS have been placed under God's feet, including him and his vast army of little devils. Satan knows he does not stand much of a chance against a praying Christian. We will study prayer in more depth in Chapter Ten.

The third most powerful weapon we have at our disposal is the *WORD OF GOD*. When Jesus was tempted by the devil in the desert, He refuted Satan with Scriptural truth. Jesus knew what the Word of God said and he used it as a weapon. Satan was no match for the Word of God and eventually ran away defeated. When our prayers contain the Word of God as we plea for protection against our enemy, he runs away with his tail between his legs, totally overtaken by a greater force.

Remember rule #2 of warfare? *USE YOUR WEAPONS*. In order for these weapons to work, we must not only use them but we must trust in their ability to protect us. Faith, prayer and the Word of God are only powerful if we use them.

Within ourselves we are weak and helpless; apart from Him we can do nothing. But with God and the powerful weapons we have in our arsenal, we can stand firm as we watch our enemy's arrows miss their target and burn out. We are more than conquerors and have won the victory!!

DAY FIVE: PRAISE AND PRACTICUM

This week we've studied the different meanings of the word *'power.'* We've compared God's power with Satan's power and learned Satan is only as powerful in our lives as we let him. God has real, genuine, authentic power, while Satan's power is make believe at best.

We've looked at Satan's psychological and physical weapons. We've looked at the weapons every believer has at his disposal, and learned as long as we remain in Christ, we are forever shielded from the enemy's fiery darts. This victorious position must be accepted by faith and is maintained by prayer and reading the Word of God. We are able to stand our ground, to stand firm and to stand strong against the schemes of the one who desperately tries to lure us out of our protective circle.

For today's praise session, let's read Psalm 121 interactively. As we look to God for help in times of spiritual attack, he promises to never sleep or slumber as He watches over us.

1. <u>Read Psalm 121</u>

   - What is the theme of this Psalm?
   - How does this Psalm make you feel?
   - Are there conditions under which the believer experiences this protection?
   - What are they?

For our practicum today, think about your life and answer the following questions:

   - Can you recall a time when you experienced spiritual warfare?
   - How did you achieve victory over our enemy?
   - Is there an area of your life right now where you may be experiencing spiritual warfare?

- What weapon is the enemy using to defeat you?

- Are you allowing Satan to bully or lure you into believing something or doing something you know is wrong?

- What are the weapons at your disposal that will defeat him?

- What do you need to do in order to use them?

Ladies, I hope this lesson has made you more aware of the heavenly realm in which we live, as well as the battle constantly taking place from within. Just as our husbands must be 'battle ready' at all times, so must we. More importantly, I hope you are encouraged to know the war is already won and we are the victors!

I pray from this day forward you will live your life to the fullest according to God's will and not be hindered by our adversary. God has provided us with protection on all sides. He has provided us with power through the working of the Holy Spirit. He has provided us with a position of victory. He leads us into battle fully armed and prepared to stand firm and hold our position. With faith, prayer and the Word of God we are more than conquerors!

Week Nine

Unity In Diversity

"The body is a unit, though it is made up of many parts; and though all its parts are many, they form one body."

1 Corinthians 12:12

As wives of warriors, diversity of all kinds becomes an integral part of our lives. Due to the global presence of United States Armed Forces, the diversity we encounter on a daily basis includes cultural, racial, and religious diversity.

We have the exceptional opportunity to meet people from all over the world. At every military base, post, or station, there are people from a variety of countries and backgrounds with whom our lives become quickly entwined. In the past sixteen years I have had neighbors from Thailand and friends with adopted Asian children. While doing a remote assignment in Korea, my husband became very good friends with natives of the country.

In the Military Chapel we experience religious diversity as well as cultural diversity. At every Chapel the services and programs offered are multi-denominational, with extra attention paid to the denominational mix of the Chaplains. We have served with Chaplains from every Protestant denomination: Methodist, Lutheran, Reformed Presbyterian, Assemblies of God, Church of Christ, and Baptist. (I'm sure I have unintentionally left a few denominations out of this list.) Personally, I have found this to be very enriching.

One principle I have learned through such experiences of diversity is that as Christians we may come in many different colors, shapes, and sizes, but we all represent the body of Christ. We are one in Him. We have all been given the same Spirit, with one goal and one purpose for our lives—that being to advance the Gospel of Jesus Christ.

This week we will explore the principle of unity in diversity. We will take a close look at the term *'unity'* and learn what it means from a Biblical perspective. Unity is a difficult concept to grasp. A simplistic view can cause rigid lines of demarcation which are then artificially imposed, whereas the broader view tends to take us in the opposite direction of an acceptable definition of unity.

Let's begin our study on this exciting principle! As always, the more we know and understand, the more our beliefs, attitudes and actions will be effected. God put together a marvelous plan from which His work is to be accomplished by making us all different. To understand the concept of unity in diversity is to free us from hindering this work as we sit back and watch Him do great and mighty things!

DAY ONE: PRAISE

Our praise time this week is going to start out a little bit differently than the previous weeks. Let's praise God for giving us our sisters and brothers in Christ.

Paul notoriously began most of his letters by thanking God for his fellow believers. He thanked God for their faithfulness, he thanked God for their fruitfulness in ministry and he thanked God for their fondness for each other.

As you read these verses interactively, join Paul in thanking God for those individuals He has given you to be co-laborers in the faith. Thank Him for those who are presently serving with you at your duty location. Thank Him for those dear sisters of the past who he allowed into your life at just the right time and perhaps you have not seen in years. And thank God also for those sisters with whom you may not see eye to eye, thus the focus on this lesson.

Ladies, as we look at the big picture, it's exciting to see so many people serving God in so many different ways. God's work and word are being spread throughout the world. Let's thank God for each other!

1. <u>Read the following verses:</u>

    - Romans 1:8–10
    - 1 Corinthians 1:4–10
    - Philippians 1:3–11
    - Colossians 1:3–8
    - 1 Thessalonians 1:2,3
    - 2 Thessalonians 1:3,4
    - Philemon 1:4–7
    - What is the underlying theme of these verses?
    - How will praying similar heart felt prayers for each other effect our actions towards one another?
    - Lists the gifts God has given some of your sisters in Christ?
    - How is God using these women to accomplish His work in and through their lives?
    - Complete this time by praising God for these people and make a covenant with God to be an encourager to them, building them up in their ministry.

DAY TWO: THE PRINCIPLE

The Biblical principle we will study this week is: *'God gives each of us a different part to play within the body of Christ. All parts are vital to the body if it is to function as one.'*

Ladies, let's jump right into the study!

1. <u>Read 1 Corinthians 12:12–31; Romans 12:4–8</u>

   - List some of the differences within the body of Christ.

   - How is each part of the body of Christ assigned?

   - Are all parts of our physical body noticeable and within sight?

   - What are some of the parts of the body of Christ that are invisible?

   - What does Scripture say about the importance of these invisible parts?

   - Where does the unity lie in all of this diversity?

   - Have we been created to be the same?

   - Can we willingly accept those who are different from us?

Unity. We must understand the Biblical concept of unity before we can engage wholeheartedly in celebrating our differences.

According to Webster's New Dictionary, the word unity means, *'the state of being one.'* As we think about this definition, we automatically think of *'sameness.'* Sameness means just that—we must all be the same, we must all be alike. We must think alike, act alike, talk alike, dress alike and worship alike. We get the idea that in order for us to have unity, we must all be the same.

This very simplistic view divides people rather than bring them together. We want everybody to be like us and have trouble accepting people who are not. Even though we know we cannot all be the same and we consciously deny any attempt to make people like us, we still do it.

We think we can only have unity if we are all Baptist, Catholics, speak in tongues, etc. We try to allow others to be what they are, but we are really very uncomfortable around people who are different than us. When we think of unity in these terms, we will never understand and embrace the Biblical concept of unity.

At the time of this writing I have become aware of a situation all too common in our churches today. This particular church offers two Sunday morning worship services. The 8:30 service is more contemporary in its worship style while the 11:00 service leans towards the more traditional Protestant worship style. According to the Pastor of the church these are two distinctly different services with two completely different congregations.

During the summer the church held a Patriotic Service in which our nations veterans were honored. The two services were combined for this special event. Much to the pastor's disappointment and dismay, many of the members who attend the more traditional service actually got up and left when contemporary Praise and Worship songs were being sung. Several long time church members left the church altogether because of the decision to start the more contemporary worship service one year earlier.

I wish I could tell you this was an exception to our all loving and all accepting Christian community. For anyone who has been involved in a church for any length of time, sadly, we know this is the norm, more than the exception.

We find the same idea of unity in marriages. We know our spouses are different from us. We are different physically, emotionally, and psychologically. Yet, we get the idea that unless the husband and wife think alike, there cannot be unity. Satan has had a field day with this definition of unity. Consequently, marriages fall apart by the thousands.

My husband calls this view of unity, 'chalk unity.' In a piece of chalk every molecule is exactly the same. Every molecule is exactly like all the others. There is no difference, no variation, no separation of each molecule. This is called a unity of composition and is the definition most of us think about when we talk about unity.

However, the Biblical definition of unity is found in 1 Corinthians 12:12.

2. Re-read 1 Corinthians 12:12

This verse introduces a definition of unity that is completely opposite of the one we have just studied. Biblical unity includes elements of diversity for the purpose of one function. Although made up of many parts, the body moves as one, with one specific goal: to bring non-believers into the saving knowledge of Jesus Christ and to uplift and edify believes. To this end, the parts must move together, totally in sync, as the engine of a well-oiled machine.

God designed us diversely so that we can reach a diverse world. Praise God He has given us each different gifts and talents. How boring and ineffective we would be if we were all the same. If God wanted 'chalk unity' among people, he would have made us all the same. We would all look alike, act alike, and think alike. We would be totally the same in composition and make up.

It is essential to broaden our view of unity to include a unity of function and purpose. We must give people who hold to the foundational unity of Jesus Christ the right to express their love and devotion to Him in a variety of ways. To say we must all be the same in our worship and expression of our faith is to deny the spiritual body concept introduced in Corinthians.

Next, let's take a closer look at our spiritual differences and how they came to be.

3. <u>Read 1 Corinthians 12:11,18; Romans 12:6</u>

    •   Do we have the opportunity to pick and choose what part we want play in the body of Christ?

    •   Who determines this?

    •   By what does he appoint each person's gifts and talents?

4. <u>Read 1 Corinthians 12:4–7</u>

    •   Why have we (God's people) been given such a variety of gifts?

    •   Are we to use our gifts to honor ourselves or to honor God?

    •   For whose benefit are we given gifts?

Clearly, we see God gives each one of us special skills and talents, gifts and abilities. They are given to each of us according to His sovereignty and grace. We did not ask for the gifts He gives us. He bestows them upon us as He sees fit for the common good of all believers.

No man is given a gift to use for his own honor, but to use for the advancement of Christianity and for the edification of believers. God entrusts us with these gifts, that we will use them for His glory.

I did not choose to be a public speaker, in fact, I purposely avoided it for most of my Christian life. Every time I was asked to give my testimony, I usually said no without a moment's hesitation. The thought of getting up in front of people and speaking was terrifying to me. Death would have been a much better option! I believed in a big God, but not one that was big enough to enable me to do that!

While attending a women's conference in 1998, I heard a woman speak who also uses a wheelchair for mobility. She ministered to many people that day, giving them hope and encouragement in Christ. I sat there with tears streaming down my face as I realized what I missed by saying 'no' to God's calling.

Determined to never say no again, I began to accept speaking engagements. Still terribly frightened before every crowd, as I remain obedient to God and His calling, He truly fills my mouth with His words. I did not choose to become a public speaker, but it clearly is what God enables me to do for Him and His people.

Many different people and many different talents. We each play a significant role in the body of Christ. No one is more important than another. The degree of visibility is not equal to the degree of importance of your gift. In fact, the less attention we receive as we play our part in the body of Christ, the more indispensable we are.

As Paul instructs us to view the body of Christ as a physical, human body, let's continue that same thought for a moment. Think about the most vital organs in your body: the heart, lungs, liver, kidneys, spleen, etc. Many, many important organs are essential for the body to function. The must each do their own special job if we are to remain healthy. Can we see these organs? Can we hold them, touch them or feel them? No. They are invisible: invisible but vital to the functioning of the human body.

So it is with the gifts God has given us. Not all of us will be the idolized arm of a professional football quarterback. Not all of us will have the legs of a speed skater, or the chest of a body builder. Think of where these people would be if it were not for the invisible workings of their vital organs?

Each of us plays an important role in the body of Christ. We were made to be different so God can use us to minister to different people. In our diversity, we must learn to function as one body, with the same spirit, the same Lord and the same God. We must learn that we all have the same goal, the same purpose, the same end to which we all must run with tolerance and perseverance for one another.

Of all these gifts, the greatest is love. Accept each other's differences, appreciate the fact that we are not all alike and always acknowledge the fact that the same spirit, the same Lord and the same God made us all!!

DAY THREE AND FOUR: THE PROOF OF THE PRINCIPLE

Yesterday we learned the Biblical definition of *'unity'* does not mean that we must all be the same in composition, but that we are all different parts which make up one body, that being the body of Jesus Christ. We are to be unified in our function and purpose as believers, working to advance the Kingdom of God. Each one of us plays a different, but important role in this work

Today, we will look at other Biblical illustrations that represent the proof of this principle.

1. <u>Read Ephesians 4:1–16</u>

    - Observe in verse three, the phrase, 'make every effort.' Is this an option or a command?

    - Whose responsibility is it to keep the unity of Christ from being broken?

    - List all the things in which we are one?

    - Again, how are gifts distributed? Read Ephesians 3:7,8

    - For what purpose are they given?

    - What is our ultimate goal as the body of Christ?

    - Verses 14–16 speak of maturity and unity. What is a necessary ingredient for this process to occur?

Whew! It is our responsibility to keep the unity of the Spirit through the bond of peace! A tall order when our differences divide us on every side.

However, Paul is very emphatic with this command. This is not an option for the Christian. The word for *'make every effort'* in Greek is *'spudadzo' and* means *'to hasten, to exert one's self.'* (Strong) We are not only supposed to keep the unity of the Spirit through the bond of peace, we are supposed to 'bust a gut' to do so. Many times this requires exertion on our part.

Why was Paul telling this so emphatically to the Ephesians? The letter to the Ephesians does not address a particular issue or problem in the church, as most of Paul's letters do, but rather Paul writes this letter to educate believers so they may have a full understanding of God's eternal purposes. Ephesians 1:10 tells us God's ultimate will is 'to be put into effect when the times will have reached their fulfillment—to bring all things in heaven and on earth together under one head, even Christ.'

Paul presents the church as the invisible body of Christ, of which Christ is the head. The division between Jews and Gentiles was deep. Gentiles were considered outsiders from the standpoint of the Mosiac Covenant. Through the blood of Christ however, they were brought near and a new humanity was born. Jews and Gentiles together—making up one humanity.

2. <u>Read Ephesians 2:11–23</u>

- What position were the Gentiles in before Christ?
- What did Christ abolish on the cross?
- What was God's purpose in doing this?
- What did Jesus put to death on the cross?
- How did he do this?
- What is the unity of the members of God's household based on?
- What does 'joined together' mean in verse 21?

Isn't this exciting? Two different people, opposite in belief and practice, hostile and separate from one another, brought together by the blood of Jesus. Jesus destroyed the dividing wall of hostility and brought peace, making one body, having access to God through one Spirit.

The first half of Ephesians tells us what God has done. The second half tells us what we must do. Beginning with Ephesians 4:1, we read we must make every effort to keep the unity of this Spirit. No more divisions, no more separations, no more hostility between each other. We must keep the unity of the Spirit through the bond of peace.

God gives a rich diversity of gifts so believers can continue to work out the purposes of God in their practical daily lives. These gifts were given to minister to each other and to build each other up as the body of Christ, promoting unity and maturity.

Ladies, *we need each other!* We need each other's gifts, talents and abilities. We need to encourage each other, drawing near to each other, forgiving each other with love and forbearance.

So what if people chose to worship differently than you? So what if there are organizational differences among denominations? So what if there are Methodists, Baptists and Reformed Presbyterians at your Bible study? We are all one in the same Spirit, one in same Lord and one in the same God. We are the body of Christ.

DAY FIVE: PRAISE AND PRACTICUM

Whew! What an exciting lesson! We've learned the Biblical concept of unity. We've come to appreciate our diversity among other believers. We may all be different but we have one function and one purpose—to glorify God and edify believers!

For our Praise time today read the following verses:

1. Read Romans 15:1–13

    •   To what does Paul refer when he uses the terms 'weak' and 'strong?'

    •   What is our purpose in not doing that which pleases ourselves?

    •   What has God given us that enables us to pursue unity among fellow believers?

- Why should we accept one another?

- What brought the Jews and the Gentiles together?

- Can the same Spirit bring together the Christians who have divisions among them?

For our Practicum today, we are going to look at three ways we can implement the Biblical principle of unity in diversity. Our goal is to promote unity and maturity in the Spirit. Let's look at some practical actions we can take to make this happen.

1. Pray for each other.

The introduction of almost every letter begins with Paul thanking God for the believers to whom he was writing. He states many times that he continually lifts them up in prayer. I believe prayer for each other bridges the gulf of even the deepest divide.

Although we may not agree with HOW each of us minister and worship, we should be thankful that God's work is being accomplished to reach people we could never reach ourselves.

Praying for others brings a sense of unity and closeness to the body of Christ. When we honestly seek God's best for each other, we are able to accept each other, in spite of our differences. If you feel somewhat left out from other church members, pray for them. See if it does not make you feel more connected to them.

- Think of someone you can pray for today who is totally different from you.

- Earnestly pray that they would know the full riches Christ intends for them. (Ephesians 1:18)

- Does this make you feel more connected to them, as part of one body?

2. Consider other believers your sisters and brothers.

We read in Acts 28:11–15, as Paul journeyed on to Rome he stopped in several places along the way. Some 'brothers' met them and invited them to spend a week with them. He mentions that the 'brothers' in

Rome were there to meet Paul and his companions. Paul was greatly encouraged at the sight of these men.

Was Paul acquainted with these men before he met them? No. But notice he called them 'brothers' and felt an immediate bond to them. The word for 'brother' in the King James Version is 'brethren.' The word 'brethren' in Greek is 'adelphos' which means, 'a fellow believer, united to another by the bond of affection, belonging to the same people.' (Strong)

As Christians, we belong to the same people. We are united in Christ, brought together by a bond of affection. How many times have you arrived at a new location, not knowing a soul, but feeling an immediate connection to fellow believers? This bond creates a unity that overcomes our differences.

- Can you think of those who are different from yourself as your sister or brother in Christ?

- Is anything in particular hindering you from accepting others into the family of God?

- How will viewing others as your sisters or brothers in Christ change the way you act towards them?

3.   Encourage one another.

Paul continually encouraged believers to encourage one another. We need each other. We need each other's gifts, talents and abilities. The Lord has blessed us all with something we can do for the benefit of others. Use your gifts to edify your sisters and brothers in Christ and allow them to use theirs to build you up.

- Can you think of someone you are not encouraging to use their gifts because they are different from yours?

- Can you appreciate the difference in each other's gifts?

- How will encouraging others to use their gifts make you feel united with them?

Ladies, this brings us to a close for this lesson. This has been a great lesson, one that is desperately needed in today's church. I pray the Holy Spirit will enable us all to be more accepting of those who are different from us. Remember, we are all one body, made from the same Spirit, the same Lord and the same God. Praise God!!

Week Ten

Plugged Into The Power

"Now unto Him who is able to do immeasurably more than all we ask or imagine, according to his power that is at work within us, to him be the glory in the church and in Christ Jesus throughout all generations, for ever and ever! Amen!"

Ephesians 3:20

I have saved this week's lesson for the very last chapter in this study for one specific reason: it is the most important lesson in the entire study and probably the most important lesson in our entire lives. This lesson is about cultivating a love relationship with the Lord Jesus Christ and surrendering ourselves unto His Lordship. We will experience the power of the Holy Spirit in our lives to the degree we embrace these two elements of our faith.

The Biblical principle in this lesson revolves around several disciplines we must dive into if we are going to receive this power through our relationship with Christ. God desires to become our bridegroom. Nothing gives Him more joy and delight than to watch his bride remain in Him through prayer, obedience and reading His word.

The proof of the principle in this lesson revolves around three specific attitudes we must accept if we are going to surrender ourselves unto His Lordship: a heart fully committed; a heart of humility; and a heart confident in Christ. These attitudes go against every grain of our human logic, reasoning and understanding and are totally backwards from the principles of the world in which we live today. Where the world thrives on its own intellect and strength, Christians are told "God opposes the proud, but gives grace to the humble." (James 4:6)

In this lesson we will learn how to be plugged into and receive the *'Dunamis'* power we learned about in Chapter Eight. This is the power that is given to every believer so we can live a life that pleases and honors God. This is the power that enables us to bear fruit in all things, showing ourselves to be Christ's disciples.

As wives of warriors, we need this power!! The physical exhaustion, mental fatigue and overwhelming circumstances we face on a daily basis can all be overcome with this power. This is not power we possess within ourselves, but power we possess by virtue of our relationship with Jesus Christ.

So Ladies, let's get on with the lesson. May the Holy Spirit renew, refresh and re-invigorate your relationship with the Bridegroom.

DAY ONE: PRAISE

We are going to begin this week's lesson with praise by reading Psalm 119. Yes, I know the Psalm has one hundred seventy six verses in it! Therefore, today we will read the first half and save the last half of the Psalm for our praise reading on day five.

There is simply no other Psalm that declares the magnificence of God's Word like Psalm 119. It is the major theme of the Psalm with all but five verses referring to it. In total, there are nine different titles used throughout the chapter that pertain to God's Word.

This Psalm is more than twice as long as other chapters. It is divided into twenty-two parts, each beginning with a letter of the Hebrew alphabet and containing eight verses. Thus, the one hundred seventy six verses! Today, we call this style of writing an acrostic and use it as a teaching tool to facilitate remembering what we have just read or heard.

My husband often uses acrostics in his sermons. Consequently, I can still remember quite a few of them.

The Psalmist's love for God and His Word and for its ability to guide and direct our lives is evident in every verse. The Word is held in high esteem and is presented with honor and excellence as the authority by which we should live our lives. In verse eleven, the Psalmist tells us the Word hidden in our heart will keep us from sin.

In verse eighty-nine, he recognizes the Word of God is eternal. Jesus said himself, "Heaven and Earth shall pass away, but my words will never pass away." (Matt. 24:35) In verse ninety-nine, he tells us God teaches us more through His Word than our human teachers could ever think about teaching us.

In verse one hundred five, the Psalmist tells us God's Word lights up our path. With God's Word continually in front of us we are never stuck floundering in the darkness. You have to love verse one hundred thirty: "The unfolding of your word gives light and understanding to the simple." Even those of us who do not have the minds of a rocket scientist are able to understand the Word of God!

Later on this week we will learn being plugged into the power of God is directly related to being plugged into the Word of God. The more we are plugged into His Word, the more we will experience His power in our lives. Hebrews 4:12 tells us "the Word of God is living and active. Sharper than any double edged sword, it penetrates even to dividing soul and spirit, joints and marrow; it judges the thoughts and attitudes of the heart." Its power in our lives is not to be underestimated!

During the course of this study, I pray you have developed a new love and discipline for reading the Bible. I agree with the Psalmist that it is to be honored, respected and treated with high regard. It brings satisfaction to our souls and hope to our hearts.

Through reading and studying God's word we come to know Him better. He reveals himself to us as our Creator, our Commander and our Comforter. We know for certain the One in whom we put our trust and our treasure.

So Ladies, let's begin this study!

1. <u>Read the first 88 verses of Psalm 119 interactively</u>

    • List the nine names for the Word that you find throughout this Psalm

- What are some of the results of meditating on God's Word?

- How does the Psalmist express his love for God?

- Memorize, or write down your favorite verse that addresses each of the following topics:
  - o The Psalmist's love for God's Word
  - o A promise of God's Word to those who love it
  - o A promise of God's Word to those who don't
  - o The reasons for his afflictions
  - o Actions the Psalmist takes to obey God's Word

That's it for today Ladies. My prayer is that our love for the Scriptures will become as deep and intense as this Psalmists. I'm excited about the rest of this lesson as we discover just how necessary spending time in God's Word is to experiencing His awesome power. Let's move on!

Day Two: The Principle

This week's principle is: *'We experience the power of the Holy Spirit in our lives to the degree we are united with Christ.'*

First, let's refresh our memories concerning what we learned about the word *'power'* in Chapter Eight on Spiritual Warfare. In Greek, the word for power is *'dunamis.'* This word means *'inherent power, power residing in a thing by virtue of its nature.'* (Strong) This is the power God has given to Jesus Christ.

1. Read Ephesians 1:19,20

God did not give this power to each of us individually, however, He did give this power to His son. Therefore, our access to and ability to receive it is dependant upon our union with Jesus Christ.

According to Webster, the word *'united'* means *'to become one, to be joined with, connected.'* We must be joined with Christ and connected *to* Him if we are going to receive God's *'dunamis'* power *through* Him.

God has given us the perfect word picture that describes this union in John 15.

2. <u>Read John 15:1–17</u>

- How is our union with Jesus described in these verses?

- What disciplines are required of us in order that we might bear fruit?

- What happens when the branch is separated from the vine?

Jesus is the vine and we are the branches. The vine gives the branches life and enables them to bear fruit. If the branch is separated from the vine, it shrivels up and dies. Apart from the vine, the branch can do nothing. If we are going to experience the power of the Holy Spirit in our lives, we must be connected to the vine!

This may seem like a given to some, but it is obvious from seeing our life long struggle with discouragement, disappointment and despair that there is a difference in just believing in God and being connected to him. As a young girl, I always believed in God. But it was not until I was connected to Him that I began to experience his wonderful power at work in my life.

I am paralyzed from the waist down. Whenever a child asks me why I cannot walk, a simple explanation which always seems to satisfy them is, "my legs don't work!" They don't work because the nerves that control my muscles are not connected to my spinal cord. They have been completely severed, cut off from the power source. There is no internal union with the nerves and my spinal cord. My legs are still attached to my body, but they are not connected to the source of the power.

The same principle applies to us as believers. We can be attached to a body of believers, but not connected to Christ. If we want to experience the power of God in our lives, we must be plugged into the source!

As we look at John 15:1–17, we notice several disciplines we are told we must dive into if we are going to experience the full measure of God's power in our lives. Since we read Psalm 119 yesterday and became familiar with the acrostic form of writing, we are going to look at these disciplines in the form of an acrostic that spells the word POWER: Prayer, Obedience, Word of God, Every branch must bear fruit, and Remain in Him.

PRAYER
Read John 15:7; John 14:13,14; 1 Thessalonians 1:2,3; Philippians 4:6,7; Colossians 4:2-4

- What are your observations of prayer from these verses?
- Does God always grant us everything we ask for in our prayers?

If we are going to be plugged into the power source, we must develop an active prayer life. An effective prayer is the fruit of a relationship with Jesus Christ.

The apostle Paul gives many examples of prayers for us to follow. His prayers are woven with praise and thanksgiving, often with others in mind. A close study of his prayers also reveals he prayed most often for things eternal, not for things temporal.

When we too, pray for things eternal, God promises to answer that prayer. God promises to give us unlimited resources so that we may accomplish His work. Too often our prayers are dominated by requests to make our lives more comfortable in the here and now, rather than on asking for eternal blessings.

I once led a Bible study I was clearly unprepared to lead. The material was far too advanced for my level of Biblical knowledge at that time.

"Who was going to quit first," I wondered. "Myself or the poor, helpless souls who were in the class?" Sensing my inadequacy to teach this class, most of them were ready to walk out after the first two weeks!

Instead of walking out, God put it on the hearts of two women to meet with me once a week to pray for the study. Faithfully, we prayed week after week that God would give us all a Spirit of wisdom and revelation as we dug deep inside His word. We prayed for each member of the class by name, that God would strengthen them in their spiritual walk.

Oh, the miracles we saw God do in the lives of those women during that study!! Not physical miracles, but Spiritual miracles. We all grew by leaps and bounds in our faith as we came to know first hand the value of an eternal prayer and the difference it makes in our lives.

OBEDIENCE
Read John 15:10; John 14:21,23,24; 1 John 2:5,6

- How is God's love made complete in us?
- How can we show God we love Him?
- In what ways has God blessed your obediance to Him?

We simply cannot experience God's power in our lives if we are not obedient to him. Obedience and love cannot be separated. It is our love for God that compels us to obey Him.

When we can grasp the truth of how much God loved us by sending Jesus to die for our sins, providing a way for us to enter into His presence, our love for Him will be an outpouring of our gratitude to Him. We will desire to zealously obey Him.

We must understand we are not placed on this earth to do whatever pleases us but to do that which pleases God. Jesus had one purpose for his life: to do the will of the one who sent him. Jesus embraced this purpose wholeheartedly with total surrender. Why? Because he loved the Father and desired to obey him with his heart, soul and mind.

We too, are commanded to love God with our heart, mind and soul. This love will manifest itself in our obedience to Him. It's through the discipline of obedience to God that we will receive His power for our lives.

WORD OF GOD
Read Colossians 3:16; Romans 10:17; Hebrews 4:12; 2 Timothy 3:16

- How do these verses describe the Word of God?
- How is our faith increased?
- How does reading God's word enable you to live more confidently in Christ?

We spent a long time yesterday during our time of praise reading about God's word. It is through the discipline of reading our Bibles that keeps us plugged into the power.

Believers cannot bear fruit in a vacuum. We cannot bear fruit apart from knowing God's word. Nowhere do I read in Scripture that once we are united with Christ, we can depart from Him and grow and mature as a Christian. If we are going to be plugged into His power so that we can live fruitful lives, we must be plugged into His word.

God is always speaking to us, however in order for us to hear Him, we must listen for Him. We listen for Him by reading and studying our Bibles. We must train our ears to hear Him through Scripture as He reveals Himself to us by the Holy Spirit. Our ears hear what they are trained to hear.

Our first duty assignment was at Nellis AFB in Las Vegas, Nevada. Since gambling is legal in that state, slot machines are placed in every entrance to every store, hoping to entice the customers to stop and play the game. There were usually several people lined up in front of those machines, fervently pulling on the handles, hoping to win the big jackpot.

Much to my surprise, some of them actually did win. As their winnings fell into the tin container at the bottom of the machine, the sound of the coins reverberated throughout the entranceway. I became very accustomed to hearing this sound as I entered every store.

I'll never forget the first time I entered a store at our next duty location in a state where gambling was not legal, hence, no slot machines. But as I entered the store, I heard the familiar clanging of coins dropping into a tin container. "Someone just won the big one," was the only thought that entered my mind.

I suddenly reminded myself I was not in Las Vegas any more! That was not the sound of coins dropping out of a slot machine. I turned around and saw the Coca-Cola man emptying the coins from a Coca-Cola vending machine! My ears had become trained to hear that sound simply because I heard it all the time.

The same principle applies to hearing the word of God. We must train our ears to hear God and we do that by reading and studying our Bibles. As we quietly listen to God through His word, He gives us the power to do that which He calls us to do.

EVERY BRANCH MUST BEAR FRUIT
Read John 15:1–5,16; Galatians 5:22,23; Colossians 1:3-13

- List the various fruits mentioned in these verses
- How are we able to bear this fruit?

The purpose of the believer is to bear fruit—fruit that will last. Gifts are given, but our fruits are produced. No matter who we are, we are all commanded to bear fruit; fruit that can only be produced by God. We must allow the Holy Spirit to develop these fruits within us. The Christian character that exhibits love, joy, peace, patience, kindness, goodness, faithfulness, gentleness and self-control is a result of being plugged into the power of God.

As we produce fruit, we are pruned so that we will produce even more fruit! The work of the Holy Spirit in our life is progressive, always working to take us to the next level in our relationship with Jesus Christ.

The more we are plugged into the power, the more fruit we will produce.

REMAIN IN CHRIST
Read John 15:5,9

- Describe how you have experienced God's power in your life by remaining in Him?
- Has there ever been a time when you tried to do something without Him?
- What were the results?

We must remain in Christ if we expect to receive the power of the Holy Spirit. Quite simply, apart from Him, we can do nothing! A branch that is not connected to the vine is lifeless. If we are not connected with Christ, we too, are lifeless.

If you have a house-plant, I'd like for you to cut off one of its leaves. Keep it around for a few days and observe what happens to it once it is no longer connected to the plant. The leaf slowly turns brown, withers up and eventually dies. It lost its power source and cannot survive on its own.

The same principle applies to believers. We have no power apart from our union and fellowship with Christ. We must remain connected to the vine if we expect to receive its power.

Let's review our acrostic: Prayer, Obedience, Word of God, Every branch must bear fruit, and we must Remain in Christ. When we practice each one of these disciplines, God promises to give us the power we need to accomplish everything He has called us to do.

So ladies, let's praise God we are connected to him, we are living in him, and we are united with him. In Him we move and live and have our being!

DAY THREE AND FOUR: THE PROOF OF THE PRINCIPLE

Yesterday we looked at various disciplines we must dive into in order to experience God's power in our lives. Today we are going to spend our time looking at three attitudes we must accept if we are to experience God's power.

Unlike the disciplines we studied about yesterday that can be measured by the actions we take, these attitudes have to do primarily with the condition of our hearts. They have to do with the priorities we set in our lives, the motives and purposes for which we live. This is where the rubber meets the road in our Christian lives.

The three attitudes of which I speak are: (1) A heart that is fully committed, (2) A heart that is confident in Christ, and (3) A heart with humility.

Let's look at the first attitude.

1. **A heart that is fully committed.**
   Read 2 Chronicles 16:9; Proverbs 23:26; 1 Kings 8:61; Jeremiah 29:13

   • Describe a heart that is fully committed

   • What happens when we seek God with all our hearts?

The King James Version of 2 Chronicles 16:9 reads, 'a heart that is *perfect* towards him.' What is a heart that is perfect towards him? The word *'perfect'* in Hebrew is *'Shalem'* and means *'complete, full, peaceful.'* (Strong) A perfect heart is one in which there is no controversy with God. A perfect heart is complete, full and peaceful.

A perfect heart is a heart wholly yielded to God. A perfect heart is completely surrendered to God and His purposes. A perfect heart is one that lives, not for its own will, but for God's. "Yet not as I will, but as you will." (Matthew 26:39)

A perfect heart is one that has died to its own desires and passions. As the parable states in John 12:24, dying is a pre-requisite to bearing fruit. Just as the grains of wheat that fall to the ground must die in order to produce a full grown plant, we must die to ourselves in order to receive God's power that produces the fruits of the Spirit.

A perfect heart is NOT a sinless heart, for we know there is no such thing. God does not look for perfect people, but he does look for people whose hearts are perfect towards him. To those he promises to strengthen, to those he promises to supply all their needs, and it's to those he promises to sustain!

Let's look at the next attitude we must accept if we are to experience God's power in our lives.

2. **A heart that is confident in Christ.**
   Read Proverbs 3:3,5; John 14:1

   - For what are you trusting God right now?
   - Describe how trusting in God allows you to live with peace in your heart?

A heart that is confident in Christ is one that trusts completely in Him. There are many verses in Scripture that address the issue of trusting God. Trust in God is essential if we are going to receive His power. God's desire for us is that we learn to trust Him more.

God is Sovereign and has a purpose and a plan for our lives. "For I know the plans I have for you, declares the Lord, plans to prosper you and not to harm you, plans to give you hope and a future." (Jeremiah 29:11) He is in control of all circumstances, directing them for our good and His glory. He knows what is best for us and brings it about in His perfect time. A heart that is confident in Christ is one that knows this truth.

A heart that is not confident in Christ is one that is filled with fear. We will never experience God's power in our lives when we are frozen with fear due to a lack of trust in God. Fear stops God dead in His tracks from blessing us. As much as He desires to give us life and give it abundantly, He cannot if we are not willing to trust Him.

A heart that is confident in Christ is one that is willing to trust God, even when the circumstances of our lives don't make any sense. Trusting God allows God to give us His power to live beyond our circumstances, not below them!

3. **A heart of humility.**
   Read Philippians 2:1–11

   - How do these verses describe humility?
   - List the ways Jesus humbled himself?

First, let's take a moment to learn what humility is not: humility is *not* the same as having a low self-esteem. Humility is not going around saying a bunch of bad things about ourselves; humility is *not* allowing ourselves to be treated disrespectfully by others; and humility is *not* thinking we have nothing of value to offer to anybody or anything.

Humility is *'having a deep sense of one's own littleness.'* (Strong) As we become more and more aware of the 'big-ness' of God, we cannot help but to become more and more aware of our littleness. One of my close friends who took over a Bible study I was leading after I left remarked, "My goal is for the women to see how REALLY BIG God is." Nothing puts us in our place faster than that realization.

The world tells us it is most important to be on the move in an upward direction. When we are moving up, we are on our way to success. Strength, ability, power and control are all attributes of successful people. We put such an emphasis on these virtues we often equate a person's worth or value as a human being to how successful they have been in life. The more power and possessions people seem to have, the more highly esteemed they are in the eyes of our culture.

There is only one problem. This train of thought is exactly opposite of what Jesus taught while he was here on earth. What the Bible does say is we are to be like-minded and imitators of Jesus Christ. The creator of the universe, the one whose power is the greatest of all, could have come to earth with an entrance filled with more pomp and circumstance, splendor and glory than words can even describe. Yet, he did not.

God himself, in the form of Jesus, came to us by way of a lowly, humble birth. He chose to come unpretentiously into the very world He created. While the heavens proclaimed the glory of his presence, he lay in the manger, a helpless infant. He laid aside his infinite *'Dunamis'* to become limited like us. He is fully human. He walks and talks, feels pleasure and pain, is tried and tempted, exhibits both anger and compassion as he shares in our human experience.

As he begins his public ministry at the age of thirty, one could not help but notice he says and does everything backwards. He claims to be a king, yet desires to be a servant. He claims to be the Son of God, yet longs to 'hang out' with those of a lesser title. He claims to be rich, but has no homes, land or money. Claiming to be truth itself, he is convicted of blasphemy. He calls himself the good shepherd, yet he ends up as the sacrifice.

Jesus came, not to accomplish his own agenda or his own plans, but gave himself up for the greater good of all mankind. His selfless devotion to His Father is exhibited by his care and concern for others. No hurt is too small, no person too foul, no sin is too great. His love and compassion for people spreads through crowds faster than fire spreads through a forest on a hot, dry, windy day.

That, my friends is humility. That is what I call having a deep sense of our own littleness. And if we are going to be plugged into the power of the Holy Spirit, we must live by the littleness displayed in our Savior. We must put aside all rank and privilege. If God should bless us with any position of leadership and influence at all, we must use it only for the greater good of others.

Let's end today's lesson by reading a chapter from the Old Testament that vividly portrays the trapping of the opposite of humility: pride. We will never experience the power of God in our lives as long as we have prideful hearts. Pride has led to the downfall of many a people, leaders in particular. Let's read some other verses on pride as well.

4. <u>Read 2 Chronicles 26; Proverbs 8:13; 11:2; 16:18; 29:23</u>

- In 2 Chronicles 26:5, why did God grant Uzziah success?

- In verse 16, what led to his downfall?

- What was he going to do in the temple?

God give us all things for His glory and His glory alone. The moment we try to take that away from Him, we are walking on dangerous ground.

Burning incense in the temple of the Lord was a duty for the priests and the priests only. Because of the power and success God granted Uzziah as king, Uzziah must have felt he was above reproach and could do anything he so desired. He lost his sense of 'littleness' in the big scheme of things. He forgot who was ultimately in charge and by whose good graces he was successful in the first place.

How often we all fall into that trap! No matter how much success God gives each of us in our lives, we are never above having to obey Him at all times. We must never forget our 'littleness' as we look upon God's 'big-ness.'

Ladies, that is it for today. What a lesson!! We have learned that in order to be plugged into the power of God, we need to have a heart that is fully committed to him, a heart that is confident in Him and a heart with humility. The rewards of such are seen in the fruit we bear and the faithfulness with which we live our lives. Praise God that we are plugged into his power!

DAY FIVE: PRAISE AND PRACTICUM

For our praise time today, we are going to begin where we left off on Day One. We'll continue reading the last half of Psalm 119. After this week's lesson, I pray you read this psalm with a new understanding of how powerful God's Word is in our lives. Oh, that we would develop a love for it that matches that of the Psalmists!!

1. <u>Begin with verse of 89 and read to the end of Psalm 119.</u>

    - As on Day One, list five of your favorite verses and share them with the rest of the class.

    - What verses do you find most comforting?

    - What verses do you find most applicable to your life?

    - What verses reflect your goals as a Christian?

For our practicum today we will look closely at our lives and ask ourselves, "Are we plugged into the power?"

- What part of this lesson do you relate to the most?

- Recall a time in your life when you know you were experiencing God's power to see you through a difficult situation.

- How can you demonstrate that you are completely yielded to God and what He wants to accomplish through you, in His way and in His time?

- How can you live a life of humility as Jesus did?

- As the wife of a warrior, in whom do you put your trust?

- How does putting your confidence in Christ affect your actions?

- How has spending more time in prayer and in God's Word affected your life?

Ladies, this brings us to the end of this study. It has been my privilege and honor to spend the past ten weeks with you. We've been all around the Bible, jumping in and out of people's lives, gleaning Biblical principles along the way.

Apply these principles to your lives. Our circumstances may change but the Biblical principles we apply to our lives will always remain the same. Let God love you as much as He so desires. Allow Him to bless you freely as you follow Him faithfully.

During the course of this study my prayer for you has been and continues to be 'that you would be encouraged in heart and united in love, so that you may have the full riches of complete understanding, in order that you may know the mystery of God, namely Christ, in who are hidden all the treasures of wisdom and knowledge.' (Colossians 2:2,3)

God Bless you, wives of the warriors! As you continue on with your military journey, may you continue to live confidently in Christ!

Becoming Connected To Christ

*A*s we have learned in this study, if we are to live confidently in Christ, we must be connected to Christ. There are many ways people try to connect with Christ. Some people think if they are basically a good person they are connected to Him. Some people think if they attend church regularly, they are connected to Him.

While these are admirable character traits we would all be wise to strive for, in themselves, they fall short of being the bridge that makes the connection. We are still separated from God. You see, there is a gap between God and mankind and it's called sin. Because of sin we are kept from God. The Bible says:

> *For all have sinned, and come short of the glory of God;*
>
> *(ROM 3:23)*

Because of our sin, we are separated from God. We must turn away from our sins and to God (repentance). You might say that becoming connected to Christ is as simple as A.B.C.

A. ADMIT TO BEING A SINNER.

Step number one is to accept the fact that there is a problem. We are sinners and we can't change that by ourselves. There are things in our lives that are wrong and we must want to make them right. We must agree with God and the Bible that we are separated from Him.

B. BELIEVE IN JESUS CHRIST.

He died for us and was raised from the dead so that we can be SAVED. (Rom. 10:9) If He didn't do this, our sins could not be forgiven. Because of Christ paying the price for salvation we can turn away from our sins and receive ETERNAL LIFE asking Him to be our Lord. He is the only way. This must be understood.

C. CONFESS JESUS AS LORD.

We must confess with our mouths Jesus as Lord. We must change our minds about the way we have lived. We must call on God, surrendering all to be saved and then share this decision with others.

If you would like to be connected to Christ so that you can life confidently in Him, would you please pray this prayer?

SAMPLE PRAYER:

"Lord, I'm calling out to you now because I'm a sinner and need to be saved. I know that there is nothing I can do on my own to get to Heaven. I believe that your son Jesus died for my sins and rose again so that I might be saved. My life is full of faults and I'm sorry. Please forgive me of

If you sincerely prayed that prayer, then tell somebody about your decision. It's very important that you start your life as a Christian reading your Bible and praying to God everyday. Find a Church that you can go to every week to learn more about Jesus and the Bible. Don't forget to write today's date down somewhere to always remember when you made your choice to receive Jesus as your savior.

Spiritual Birth Certificate

By confessing with my mouth Jesus as my Lord and believing in my heart that God raised Him from the dead, I became a Christian today. I asked God to forgive me of all my sins because I was a lost sinner. Now I have Eternal Life and will be with God forever in Heaven. I'm a new person and will serve Jesus every day of my life. I have been born again. I am connected to Christ.

Date: _____

Signed: _____

Bibliography

Bonhoeffer, Dietrich. <u>Spiritual Care</u>; Fortress Press, 1985.

Bridges, Jerry. <u>Transforming Grace</u>; Navpress, 1991.

Ferguson, Sinclair B., Packer, J.I., Wright, David F. <u>New Dictionary of Theology</u>; Intervaristy Press, 1988.

Hopkins, Evan H. <u>The Law of Liberty in Spiritual Life</u>; Lowe & Brydone, LTD, 1974.

Hybels, Bill & Rob Wilkins. <u>Descending Into Greatness</u>; Zondervan Publishing House, 1993.

Lucado, Max. <u>Just Like Jesus</u>; Word Publishing, 1998.

Tozer, A. W. <u>That Incredible</u> Christian; Most of the chapters in this book appeared as editorials in <u>The Alliance Witness</u>, of which Dr. Tozer was editor during the years 1960–1963.

Willmington, Dr. H. L. <u>Willmington's Guide to the Bible</u>; Tyndale House Publishers, Inc., 1985.

To order additional copies of

Wives of
_____
the Warriors

Ha ve your credit card ready and call:

1-877-421-READ (7323)

or please visit our web site at
www.pleasantword.com

Also available at: www.amazon.com

Printed in the United States
20201LVS00007B/298-318